OHIO RULES OF EVIDENCE

As Revised Through July 1, 2017

ISBN-13:978-1981490981

ISBN-10: 1981490981

Gulf Coast Legal Publishing, LLC
New Orleans, Louisiana

OHIO RULES OF EVIDENCE

Article I GENERAL PROVISIONS

Article II JUDICIAL NOTICE

Article III PRESUMPTIONS

Article IV RELEVANCY AND ITS LIMITS

Article V PRIVILEGES

Article VI WITNESS

Rule

Article VII OPIONIONS AND EXPERT TESTIMONY

Article VIII HEARSAY

Article IX AUTHENTICATION AND IDENTIFICATION

Article X CONTENTS OF WRITINGS, RECORDINGS AND PHOTGRAPHS

Article XI MISCELLANEOUS RULES

ARTICLE I. GENERAL PROVISIONS

RULE 101.   Scope of Rules: Applicability; Privileges; Exceptions

(A)   Applicability. These rules govern proceedings in the courts of this state, subject to the exceptions stated in division (C) of this rule.

(B)   Privileges. The rule with respect to privileges applies at all stages of all actions, cases, and proceedings conducted under these rules.

(C)   Exceptions. These rules (other than with respect to privileges) do not apply in the following situations:

(1)   Admissibility determinations. Determinations prerequisite to rulings on the admissibility of evidence when the issue is to be determined by the court under Evid.R. 104.

(2)   Grand jury. Proceedings before grand juries.

(3)   Miscellaneous criminal proceedings. Proceedings for extradition or rendition of fugitives; sentencing; granting or revoking probation; proceedings with respect to community control sanctions; issuance of warrants for arrest, criminal summonses and search warrants; and proceedings with respect to release on bail or otherwise.

(4)   Contempt. Contempt proceedings in which the court may act summarily.

(5)   Arbitration. Proceedings for those mandatory arbitrations of civil cases authorized by the rules of superintendence and governed by local rules of court.

(6)   Other rules. Proceedings in which other rules prescribed by the Supreme Court govern matters relating to evidence.

(7)   Special non-adversary statutory proceedings. Special statutory proceedings of a non-adversary nature in which these rules would by their nature be clearly inapplicable.

(8)   Small claims division. Proceedings in the small claims division of a county or municipal court.

[Effective: July 1, 1980; amended effective July 1, 1990; July 1, 1996; July 1, 1999.]

Staff Note (July 1, 1999 Amendment)

Rule 101 Scope of Rules; Applicability; Privileges; Exceptions

Rule 101(C) Exceptions

The phrase "community control sanctions" was added to division (C)(3) of the rule in accordance with changes resulting from the adoption of Senate Bill 2, effective July 1, 1996, and in order to make the rule conform to current Ohio criminal practice.

Staff Note (July 1, 1996 Amendment)

Rule 101 Scope of Rules; Applicability; Privileges; Exceptions

Rule 101(A) Applicability

The amendment deleted the rule's reference to proceedings "before court-appointed referees and magistrates." The deleted language was redundant, since proceedings before these judicial officers are "proceedings in the courts of this state." The amendment also harmonized the statement of the rules' applicability with the usage in other rules of practice and procedure, none of which makes specific reference to particular classes of judicial officers before whom proceedings governed by the rules might be conducted. See Civ. R. 1(A), Crim. R. 19A), and Juv. R. 1(A). The amendment is intended only as a technical modification and no substantive change is intended.

RULE 102.   Purpose and Construction

The purpose of these rules is to provide procedures for the adjudication of causes to the end that the truth may be ascertained and proceedings justly determined. The principles of the common law of Ohio shall supplement the provisions of these rules, and the rules shall be construed to state the principles of the common law of Ohio unless the rule clearly indicates that a change is intended. These rules shall not supersede substantive statutory provisions.

[Effective: July 1, 1980; amended effectively July 1, 1996.]

Staff Note (July 1, 1996 Amendment)

Rule 102 Purpose and Construction; Supplementary Principles

As originally adopted, Evid. R. 102 referred to the common law of Ohio, but only as a framework for construing the particular rules within the Rules of Evidence. The original text of Rule 102 did not suggest what role, if any, the common law was to have in regard to evidentiary issues as to which the Rules of Evidence were silent.

In the years since Ohio adopted the Rules of Evidence, Ohio has added rules codifying the common law on certain topics that the rules had not addressed. Thus, for example, prior to the adoption of Evid. R. 616 in 1991, the rules contained no rule governing the impeachment of a witness for bias or interest. See Staff Note (1991), Evid. R. 616. Even after the adoption of Rule 616, other rules of impeachment remained unaddressed. See, e.g., *Ramage v. Central Ohio Emergency Serv., Inc.* (1992), 64 Ohio St. 3d 97, 110 (use of learned treatises for impeachment). Similarly, the rules do not expressly address questions regarding the admissibility of expert opinions on certain subjects. See, e.g., *Stinson v. England* (1994), 69 Ohio St. 3d 451 (expert opinion on causation is inadmissible unless the opinion is that causation is at least probable).

Omissions such as these occur across the entire body of evidence law. The Rules of Evidence, that is, are not an exhaustive compilation of the rules governing evidence questions, nor are the rules preemptive as to subjects that they do not address. The amendment makes clear in the text of the rule not only that the common law of Ohio provides a framework for construing the content of specific rules, but also that the common law provides the rules of decision as to questions not addressed by specific rules.

In addition, in the portion of the rule that establishes the common law as the basis of interpretation of specific rules, the phrase "common law" was amended to read "principles of the common law." The amendment harmonized the reference with the usage in other rules. See, e.g., Evid. R. 501. In addition, it is intended to acknowledge more clearly the character of the common law as an evolving body of principles and precedents, rather than as a static collection of tightly prescribed rules.

RULE 103.   Rulings on Evidence

(A)   Effect of erroneous ruling. Error may not be predicated upon a ruling which admits or excludes evidence unless a substantial right of the party is affected, and

(1)   Objection. In case the ruling is one admitting evidence, a timely objection or motion to strike appears of record, stating the specific ground of objection, if the specific ground was not apparent from the context; or

(2)   Offer of proof. In case the ruling is one excluding evidence, the substance of the evidence was made known to the court by offer or was apparent from the context within which questions were asked. Offer of proof is not necessary if evidence is excluded during cross-examination.

Once the court rules definitely on the record, either before or at trial, a party need not renew an objection or offer of proof to preserve a claim of error for appeal.

(B)   Record of offer and ruling. At the time of making the ruling, the court may add any other or further statement which shows the character of the evidence, the form in which it was offered, the objection made, and the ruling thereon. It may direct the making of an offer in question and answer form.

(C)   Hearing of jury. In jury cases, proceedings shall be conducted, to the extent practicable, so as to prevent inadmissible evidence from being suggested to the jury by any means, such as making statements or offers of proof or asking questions in the hearing of the jury.

(D)   Plain error. Nothing in this rule precludes taking notice of plain errors affecting substantial rights although they were not brought to the attention of the court.

[Effective: July 1, 1980; amended effective July 1, 2017.]

RULE 104.   Preliminary Questions

(A)   **Questions of admissibility generally.**   Preliminary questions concerning the qualification of a person to be a witness, the existence of a privilege, or the admissibility of evidence shall be determined by the court, subject to the provisions of subdivision (B).   In making its determination it is not bound by the rules of evidence except those with respect to privileges.

(B)   **Relevancy conditioned on fact.**   When the relevancy of evidence depends upon the fulfillment of a condition of fact, the court shall admit it upon, or subject to, the introduction of evidence sufficient to support a finding of the fulfillment of the condition.

(C)   **Hearing of jury.**   Hearings on the admissibility of confessions shall in all cases be conducted out of the hearing of the jury.   Hearings on other preliminary matters shall also be conducted out of the hearing of the jury when the interests of justice require.

(D)   **Testimony by accused.**   The accused does not, by testifying upon a preliminary matter, become subject to cross-examination as to other issues in the case.

(E)   **Weight and credibility.**   This rule does not limit the right of a party to introduce before the jury evidence relevant to weight or credibility.

[Effective: July 1, 1980; amended effectively July 1, 2007.]

RULE 105. Limited Admissibility

When evidence which is admissible as to one party or for one purpose but not admissible as to another party or for another purpose is admitted, the court, upon request of a party, shall restrict the evidence to its proper scope and instruct the jury accordingly.

[Effective: July 1, 1980.]

RULE 106.　Remainder of or Related Writings or Recorded Statements

When a writing or recorded statement or part thereof is introduced by a party, an adverse party may require the introduction at that time of any other part or any other writing or recorded statement which is otherwise admissible and which ought in fairness to be considered contemporaneously with it.

[Effective:　July 1, 1980; amended effectively July 1, 2007.]

ARTICLE II. JUDICIAL NOTICE

RULE 201.   Judicial Notice of Adjudicative Facts

(A)   Scope of rule. This rule governs only judicial notice of adjudicative facts; i.e., the facts of the case.

(B)   Kinds of facts. A judicially noticed fact must be one not subject to reasonable dispute in that it is either (1) generally known within the territorial jurisdiction of the trial court or (2) capable of accurate and ready determination by resort to sources whose accuracy cannot reasonably be questioned.

(C)   When discretionary. A court may take judicial notice, whether requested or not.

(D)   When mandatory. A court shall take judicial notice if requested by a party and supplied with the necessary information.

(E)   Opportunity to be heard. A party is entitled upon timely request to an opportunity to be heard as to the propriety of taking judicial notice and the tenor of the matter noticed. In the absence of prior notification, the request may be made after judicial notice has been taken.

(F)   Time of taking notice. Judicial notice may be taken at any stage of the proceeding.

(G)   Instructing jury. In a civil action or proceeding, the court shall instruct the jury to accept as conclusive any fact judicially noticed. In a criminal case, the court shall instruct the jury that it may, but is not required to, accept as conclusive any fact judicially noticed.

[Effective: July 1, 1980.]

ARTICLE III. PRESUMPTIONS

RULE 301.   Presumptions in General in Civil Actions and Proceedings

In all civil actions and proceedings not otherwise provided for by statute enacted by the General Assembly or by these rules, a presumption imposes on the party against whom it is directed the burden of going forward with evidence to rebut or meet the presumption, but does not shift to such party the burden of proof in the sense of the risk of non-persuasion, which remains throughout the trial upon the party on whom it was originally cast.

[Effective: July 1, 1980.]

RULE 302.   [RESERVED]

ARTICLE IV. RELEVANCY AND ITS LIMITS

RULE 401.   Definition of "Relevant Evidence"

"Relevant evidence" means evidence having any tendency to make the existence of any fact that is of consequence to the determination of the action more probable or less probable than it would be without the evidence.

[Effective: July 1, 1980.]

RULE 402. Relevant Evidence Generally Admissible; Irrelevant Evidence Inadmissible

All relevant evidence is admissible, except as otherwise provided by the Constitution of the United States, by the Constitution of the State of Ohio, by statute enacted by the General Assembly not in conflict with a rule of the Supreme Court of Ohio, by these rules, or by other rules prescribed by the Supreme Court of Ohio. Evidence which is not relevant is not admissible.

[Effective: July 1, 1980.]

RULE 403.   Exclusion of Relevant Evidence on Grounds of Prejudice, Confusion, or Undue Delay

(A)   Exclusion mandatory.   Although relevant, evidence is not admissible if its probative value is substantially outweighed by the danger of unfair prejudice, of confusion of the issues, or of misleading the jury.

(B)   Exclusion discretionary.   Although relevant, evidence may be excluded if its probative value is substantially outweighed by considerations of undue delay, or needless presentation of cumulative evidence.

[Effective: July 1, 1980; amended effective July 1, 1996.]

Staff Note (July 1, 1996 Amendment)

Rule 403 Exclusion of Relevant Evidence on Grounds of Prejudice, Confusion, or Undue Delay

The amendment modifies the title of the rule to reflect its content. As originally adopted, Evid. R. 403 varied from its federal counterpart by excluding "waste of time" as a separate or independent ground for excluding otherwise relevant and admissible evidence. The title of the Ohio rule, however, was not modified to reflect this difference between the Ohio and federal texts. The amendment substitutes "undue delay" in place of the original title's reference to "waste of time" as a ground of exclusion, so that the title will more accurately reflect the content of the Ohio text. The amendment is intended only as a technical correction; no substantive change is intended.

RULE 404.   Character Evidence not Admissible to Prove Conduct; Exceptions; Other Crimes

(A)   Character evidence generally.   Evidence of a person's character or a trait of character is not admissible for the purpose of proving action in conformity therewith on a particular occasion, subject to the following exceptions:

(1)   Character of accused.   Evidence of a pertinent trait of character offered by an accused, or by the prosecution to rebut the same is admissible; however, in prosecutions for rape, gross sexual imposition, and prostitution, the exceptions provided by statute enacted by the General Assembly are applicable.

(2)   Character of victim.   Evidence of a pertinent trait of character of the victim of the crime offered by an accused, or by the prosecution to rebut the same, or evidence of a character trait of peacefulness of the victim offered by the prosecution in a homicide case to rebut evidence that the victim was the first aggressor is admissible; however, in prosecutions for rape, gross sexual imposition, and prostitution, the exceptions provided by statute enacted by the General Assembly are applicable.

(3)   Character of witness.   Evidence of the character of a witness on the issue of credibility is admissible as provided in Rules 607, 608, and 609.

(B)   Other crimes, wrongs or acts.   Evidence of other crimes, wrongs, or acts is not admissible to prove the character of a person in order to show action in conformity therewith. It may, however, be admissible for other purposes, such as proof of motive, opportunity, intent, preparation, plan, knowledge, identity, or absence of mistake or accident. In criminal cases, the proponent of evidence to be offered under this rule shall provide reasonable notice in advance of trial, or during trial if the court excuses pretrial notice on good cause shown, of the general nature of any such evidence it intends to introduce at trial.

[Effective: July 1, 1980; amended effectively July 1, 2007, July 1, 2012.]

Staff Note (July 1, 2012 Amendment)

The original Ohio Rule did not adopt the notice requirement included in the federal version of the rule. The rule, as amended, adds mutuality to the federal version of the rule so as to also provide the prosecution with notice of the defendant's intention to offer evidence under this rule. The purpose of adding the notice requirement is to provide the prosecution and the defense with the opportunity to prepare their case. Notice provided pursuant to this rule does not constitute a "demand of the defendant" under Crim.R. 16, and does not, in and of itself, constitute the initiation of discovery under Crim.R. 16. The rule should not be construed to exclude otherwise relevant and admissible evidence solely because of a lack of notice, absent a showing of bad faith.

RULE 405. Methods of Proving Character

(A)   Reputation or opinion. In all cases in which evidence of character or a trait of character of a person is admissible, proof may be made by testimony as to reputation or by testimony in the form of an opinion. On cross-examination, inquiry is allowable into relevant specific instances of conduct.

(B)   Specific instances of conduct. In cases in which character or a trait of character of a person is an essential element of a charge, claim, or defense, proof may also be made of specific instances of his conduct.

[Effective: July 1, 1980.]

RULE 406.   Habit; Routine Practice

Evidence of the habit of a person or of the routine practice of an organization, whether corroborated or not and regardless of the presence of eyewitnesses, is relevant to prove that the conduct of the person or organization on a particular occasion was in conformity with the habit or routine practice.

[Effective: July 1, 1980.]

RULE 407.   Subsequent Remedial Measures

When, after an injury or harm allegedly caused by an event, measures are taken which, if taken previously, would have made the injury or harm less likely to occur, evidence of the subsequent measures is not admissible to prove negligence or culpable conduct in connection with the event.   This rule does not require the exclusion of evidence of subsequent measures when offered for another purpose, such as proving ownership, control, or feasibility of precautionary measures, if controverted, or impeachment.

[Effective: July 1, 1980; amended effective July 1, 2000.]

Staff Note (July 1, 2000 Amendment)

Rule 407 Subsequent remedial measures

In 1997, Federal Rule of Evidence 407 was amended in two respects. The Ohio amendment is based on the first change in the federal rule: the phrase "injury or harm allegedly caused by an" was added to clarify that a repair or remedial measure must take effect after the accident or incident being litigated in order for the rule to apply. A measure that takes effect after purchase but before the accident or incident being litigated is not a subsequent measure. *See Traylor v. Husqvarna Motor* (7th Cir. 1993, 988 F.2d 729, 733 ("The problem with applying Rule 407 was not lack of culpable conduct but the fact that the remedial measures were taken before rather than after the 'event,' which in an accident case the courts have invariably and we think correctly understood to mean the accident."); *Cates v. Sears, Roebuck & Co.* (5th Cir. 1991), 928 F.2d 679, ("The 'event' to which Rule 407 speaks is the accident, not the sale."); *Chase v. General Motors Corp.* (4th Cir. 1988), 856 F.2d 17, 21-22.

The second change to the federal rule, which involves strict liability cases, has not been adopted.

RULE 408.   Compromise and Offers to Compromise

Evidence of (1) furnishing or offering or promising to furnish, or (2) accepting or offering or promising to accept, a valuable consideration in compromising or attempting to compromise a claim which was disputed as to either validity or amount, is not admissible to prove liability for or invalidity of the claim or its amount. Evidence of conduct or statements made in compromise negotiations is likewise not admissible. This rule does not require the exclusion of any evidence otherwise discoverable merely because it is presented in the course of compromise negotiations. This rule also does not require exclusion when the evidence is offered for another purpose, such as proving bias or prejudice of a witness, negativing a contention of undue delay, or proving an effort to obstruct a criminal investigation or prosecution.

[Effective: July 1, 1980.]

RULE 409.　Payment of Medical and Similar Expenses

Evidence of furnishing or offering or promising to pay medical, hospital, or similar expenses occasioned by an injury is not admissible to prove liability for the injury.

[Effective:　July 1, 1980.]

RULE 410. Inadmissibility of Pleas, Offers of Pleas, and Related Statements

(A)   Except as provided in division (B) of this rule, evidence of the following is not admissible in any civil or criminal proceeding against the defendant who made the plea or who was a participant personally or through counsel in the plea discussions:

(1)   a plea of guilty that later was withdrawn;

(2)   a plea of no contest or the equivalent plea from another jurisdiction;

(3)   a plea of guilty in a violations bureau;

(4)   any statement made in the course of any proceedings under Rule 11 of the Rules of Criminal Procedure or equivalent procedure from another jurisdiction regarding the foregoing pleas;

(5)   any statement made in the course of plea discussions in which counsel for the prosecuting authority or for the defendant was a participant and that do not result in a plea of guilty or that result in a plea of guilty later withdrawn.

(B)   A statement otherwise inadmissible under this rule is admissible in either of the following:

(1)   any proceeding in which another statement made in the course of the same plea or plea discussions has been introduced and the statement should, in fairness, be considered contemporaneously with it;

(2)   a criminal proceeding for perjury or false statement if the statement was made by the defendant under oath, on the record, and in the presence of counsel.

[Effective: July 1, 1980; amended effective July 1, 1991.]

Staff Note (July 1, 1991 Amendment)

Rule 410 Inadmissibility of Pleas, Offers of Pleas, and Related Statements

At the time Evid. R. 410 became effective in July 1980, there was "no substantive variation between the Ohio rule and the Federal Rule." Ohio Staff Note (1980). The term "no contest" had replaced the phrase "nolo contendere" used in the federal rule and the phrases "or the equivalent plea from another jurisdiction" and "or a plea of guilty in a violations bureau" had been added to the Ohio rule.

The federal rule, however, was thereafter amended. Several federal cases had read the federal rule broadly to cover some statements made during "plea bargain" discussions between defendants and law enforcement officers. See *United States v. Harman*, 544 F. 2d 791, 795-799 (5th Cir. 1977); *United States v. Brooks*, 536 F. 2d 1137, 1138-39 (6th Cir. 1976); *United States v. Smith*, 525 F. 2d 1017, 1020-22 (10th Cir. 1975). Accordingly, the federal drafters became concerned "that an otherwise voluntary admission to law enforcement officials [might be] rendered inadmissible merely because it was made in the hope of obtaining leniency by a plea." Fed. R. Evid. 410, Advisory Committee Note (1980). Federal Rule 410 now specifies that only plea discussions with the "attorney for the prosecuting authority" are covered by the rule.

The amendment incorporates the same limitation into the Ohio rule. It is intended to clarify an area of ambiguity. The amended rule is designed to protect plea bargaining statements involving attorneys in order to promote the disposition of criminal cases by compromise. Statements made by an accused to the police are not covered by this rationale. Improper inducements by the police may be challenged under the constitutional standards governing the voluntariness of confessions, but may not be excluded under this rule.

Unlike the federal rule, the amendment specifically covers plea bargaining statements made by defense counsel. Such statements are excluded from evidence when made either to the prosecutor or the police.

Two additional changes are effected by the amendment. First, the amendment recognizes an exception in addition to the exception for perjury and false statement prosecutions. This exception applies in "any proceeding in which another statement made in the course of the same plea or plea discussions has been introduced and the statement should, in fairness, be considered contemporaneously with it." This provision is a restatement of the "rule of completeness" found in Evid. R. 106.

Second, the amendment specifically excludes "any statement made in the course of any proceedings under Rule 11 of the Rules of Criminal Procedure or equivalent procedure from another jurisdiction." This provision was added for clarification; the same result would have been reached under the old rule.

RULE 411.   Liability Insurance

Evidence that a person was or was not insured against liability is not admissible upon the issue whether the person acted negligently or otherwise wrongfully. This rule does not require the exclusion of evidence of insurance against liability when offered for another purpose, such as proof of agency, ownership or control, if controverted, or bias or prejudice of a witness.

[Effective: July 1, 1980; amended effectively July 1, 2007.]

ARTICLE V. PRIVILEGES

RULE 501.   General Rule

The privilege of a witness, person, state or political subdivision thereof shall be governed by statute enacted by the General Assembly or by principles of common law as interpreted by the courts of this state in the light of reason and experience.

[Effective: July 1, 1980.]

ARTICLE VI. WITNESSES

RULE 601.   General Rule of Competency

Every person is competent to be a witness except:

(A)   Those of unsound mind, and children under ten years of age, who appear incapable of receiving just impressions of the facts and transactions respecting which they are examined, or of relating them truly.

(B)   A spouse testifying against the other spouse charged with a crime except when either of the following applies:

(1)   a crime against the testifying spouse or a child of either spouse is charged;

(2)   the testifying spouse elects to testify.

(C)   An officer, while on duty for the exclusive or main purpose of enforcing traffic laws, arresting or assisting in the arrest of a person charged with a traffic violation punishable as a misdemeanor where the officer at the time of the arrest was not using a properly marked motor vehicle as defined by statute or was not wearing a legally distinctive uniform as defined by statute.

(D)   A person giving expert testimony on the issue of liability in any medical claim, as defined in R.C. 2305.113, asserted in any civil action against a physician, podiatrist, or hospital arising out of the diagnosis, care, or treatment of any person by a physician or podiatrist, unless:

(1)   The person testifying is licensed to practice medicine and surgery, osteopathic medicine and surgery, or podiatric medicine and surgery by the state medical board or by the licensing authority of any state;

(2)   The person devotes at least one-half of his or her professional time to the active clinical practice in his or her field of licensure, or to its instruction in an accredited school and

(3)   The person practices in the same or a substantially similar specialty as the defendant. The court shall not permit an expert in one medical specialty to testify against a health care provider in another medical specialty unless the expert shows both that the standards of care and practice in the two specialties are similar and that the expert has substantial familiarity between the specialties.

If the person is certified in a specialty, the person must be certified by a board recognized by the American board of medical specialties or the American board of osteopathic specialties in a specialty having acknowledged expertise and training directly related to the particular health care matter at issue.

Nothing in this division shall be construed to limit the power of the trial court to adjudge the testimony of any expert witness incompetent on any other ground, or to limit the power of the trial court to allow the testimony of any other witness, on a matter unrelated to the liability issues in the medical claim, when that testimony is relevant to the medical claim involved.

This division shall not prohibit other medical professionals who otherwise are competent to testify under these rules from giving expert testimony on the appropriate standard of care in their own profession in any claim asserted in any civil action against a physician, podiatrist, medical professional, or hospital arising out of the diagnosis, care, or treatment of any person.

(E)   As otherwise provided in these rules.

[Effective: July 1, 1980; amended effective July 1, 1991; July 1, 2016.]

Staff Note (July 1, 1991 Amendment)

Rule 601 General Rule of Competency
Rule 601(A) Children and mental incompetents

Evid. R. 601(A) was amended by deleting "and;"from the end of the rule. This is a technical change only.

Rule 601(B) Spouse testifying

As adopted in 1980, Evid. R. 601(B) provided that a witness was incompetent to testify against his or her spouse in a criminal case unless the charged offense involved a crime against the testifying spouse or the children of either spouse. The rule was based on the policy of protecting the marital relationship from "dissension" and the "natural repugnance" for convicting a defendant upon the testimony of his or her "intimate life partner." 8 J. Wigmore, Evidence 216-17 (McNaughton rev. 1961).

The important issue is who can waive the rule – the defendant or the witness. Under the old rule, the defendant could prevent his or spouse from testifying. In some situations the policy underlying the rule simply does not apply, but the rule does. For example, if a husband kills his mother-in-law and his wife is a witness, she could be prevented from testifying. This would be true even if they were separated and she desired to testify. Cf. *Locke v. State* (1929), 33 Ohio App. 445, 169 N.E. 833. The amendment changes this result, by permitting the wife to elect to testify.

The approach is supported by a number of commentators. As McCormick has pointed out: "The privilege has sometimes been defended on the ground that it protects family harmony. But family harmony is nearly always past saving when the spouse is willing to aid the prosecution. The privilege is an archaic survival of a mystical religious dogma and of a way of thinking about the marital relation that is today outmoded." C. McCormick, Evidence 162 (3d ed. 1984). *See also* 8 J. Wigmore, Evidence 221 (McNaughton rev. 1961) ("This marital privilege is the merest anachronism in legal theory and an indefensible obstruction to truth in practice."); Huhn, "Sacred Seal of Secrecy"; The Rules of Spousal Incompetency and Marital Privilege in Criminal Cases (1987), 20 Akron L. Rev. 433.

The 1991 amendment does not abolish the spousal incompetency rule. The spouse could not be compelled to testify if he or she did not want to testify. In January 1981, the Supreme Court proposed an amendment that would have deleted Evid. R. 601(B). 54 Ohio Bar 175 (1981). This amendment subsequently was withdrawn. 54 Ohio Bar 972 (1981). The 1991 amendment differs from the 1981 proposal. The 1981 proposal would have abolished the spousal incompetency rule in its entirety, thereby permitting the prosecution to force the spouse to testify. The 1991 amendment does not permit the prosecutor to force testimony from an unwilling spouse.

Moreover, the amendment still leaves the defendant with the protection of the confidential communication privilege, which is recognized in R.C. 2317.02(C) and R.C. 2945.42 and governed by Evid. R. 501. This privilege is not affected by Evid. R. 601(B).

Rule 601(D) Medical experts

Evid. R. 601(D) was amended to prevent the application of the rule in cases in which a physician, podiatrist, hospital, or medical professional is sued as a result of alleged negligence on the part of a nurse or other medical professional. Some cases have held that a nurse is not competent under Evid. R. 601(D) to testify about the standard of nursing care in such a case. *See Harter v. Wadsworth-Rittman* (August 30, 1989), Medina App. No. 1790, unreported, motion to certify record overruled (December 20, 1989), 47 Ohio St.3d 715, 549 N.E.2d 170.

The amendment limits the rule to claims involving care by a physician or podiatrist, and does not prohibit other medical professionals, including nurses, from testifying as to the appropriate standards of professional care in their field.

Also, the requirement that an expert medical witness devote three-fourths of his or her time to active clinical practice or instruction was reduced to at least one-half. The phrase "accredited university" was changed to "accredited school" because some accredited medical schools are not associated with a university.

Staff Notes (July 1, 2016 Amendments)

Nonsubstantive revisions are made to Evid.R. 601(D) to make clear that the rule applies only to expert testimony as to liability in any medical claim, as defined by R.C. 2305.113, asserted against a physician, podiatrist, or hospital arising out of the diagnosis, care, or treatment of any person by a physician or podiatrist. The rule does not apply to expert testimony for any other medical claims, or for any dental, optometric, or chiropractic claims, as defined by R.C. 2305.113.

The structure and provisions of Evid.R. 601(D) are also revised to more-closely resemble the structure of R.C. 2743.43 and to incorporate the provisions of that statute that are not inconsistent with the provisions of the current rule. Pursuant to authority of Article IV, Section 5(B) of the Ohio Constitution, the provisions of R.C. 2743.43 are superseded in their entirety by the amended rule.

RULE 602.　Lack of Personal Knowledge

A witness may not testify to a matter unless evidence is introduced sufficient to support a finding that the witness has personal knowledge of the matter. Evidence to prove personal knowledge may, but need not, consist of the witness' own testimony. This rule is subject to the provisions of Rule 703, relating to opinion testimony by expert witnesses.

[Effective: July 1, 1980; amended effectively July 1, 2007.]

RULE 603.   Oath or Affirmation

Before testifying, every witness shall be required to declare that the witness will testify truthfully, by oath or affirmation administered in a form calculated to awaken the witness' conscience and impress the witness' mind with the duty to do so.

[Effective: July 1, 1980; amended effectively July 1, 2007.]

RULE 604.   Interpreters

An interpreter is subject to the provisions of these rules relating to qualification as an expert and the administration of an oath or affirmation to make a true translation.

[Effective: July 1, 1980; amended effectively July 1, 2007.]

RULE 605.   Competency of Judge as Witness

The judge presiding at the trial may not testify in that trial as a witness. No objection need be made in order to preserve the point.

[Effective: July 1, 1980.]

RULE 606. Competency of Juror as Witness

(A)   At the trial. A member of the jury may not testify as a witness before that jury in the trial of the case in which the juror is sitting. If the juror is called so to testify, the opposing party shall be afforded an opportunity to object out of the presence of the jury.

(B)   Inquiry into validity of verdict or indictment. Upon an inquiry into the validity of a verdict or indictment, a juror may not testify as to any matter or statement occurring during the course of the jury's deliberations or to the effect of anything upon that or any other juror's mind or emotions as influencing the juror to assent to or dissent from the verdict or indictment or concerning the juror's mental processes in connection therewith. A juror may testify on the question whether extraneous prejudicial information was improperly brought to the jury's attention or whether any outside influence was improperly brought to bear on any juror, only after some outside evidence of that act or event has been presented. However a juror may testify without the presentation of any outside evidence concerning any threat, any bribe, any attempted threat or bribe, or any improprieties of any officer of the court. A juror's affidavit or evidence of any statement by the juror concerning a matter about which the juror would be precluded from testifying will not be received for these purposes.

[Effective: July 1, 1980; amended effectively July 1, 2007.]

RULE 607.   Impeachment

(A)   Who may impeach. The credibility of a witness may be attacked by any party except that the credibility of a witness may be attacked by the party calling the witness by means of a prior inconsistent statement only upon a showing of surprise and affirmative damage. This exception does not apply to statements admitted pursuant to Evid.R. 801(D)(1)(A), 801(D)(2), or 803.

(B)   Impeachment: reasonable basis. A questioner must have a reasonable basis for asking any question pertaining to impeachment that implies the existence of an impeaching fact.

[Effective: July 1, 1980; amended July 1, 1998.]

Staff Note (July 1, 1998 Amendment)

Rule 607 Impeachment

Rule 607(A) Who may impeach.

This paragraph was labeled division (A), a title was added, and the style used for rule references was changed. There was no substantive amendment to this division.

Rule 607(B) Impeachment: reasonable basis.

The 1998 amendment added division (B) to the rule.

A party inquiring into specific instances of conduct must have a good faith basis in fact for asking the question. E.g., *State v. Gillard* (1988), 40 Ohio St.3d 226, 231, 533 N.E.2d 272 ("[A] cross-examiner may ask a question if the examiner has a good-faith belief that a factual predicate for the question exists."), cert. denied, 492 U.S. 925, 109 S.Ct. 3263, 106 L.Ed.2d 608 (1989); *Kornreich v. Indus. Fire Ins. Co.* (1936), 132 Ohio St. 78, 88 ("These collateral attacks must be made in good faith . . . ."). This is especially true in criminal cases where the unfair prejudice may be great. See also 1 McCormick, Evidence § 41, at 140 (4th ed. 1992) ("A good faith basis for the inquiry is required."). Professor Graham explains the requirement as follows:

> Note that the requirement of a good faith basis applies only when the cross-examiner is effectively asserting in the form of a question the truth of a factual statement included within the question. If the cross-examiner is merely inquiring whether something is or is not true, a good faith basis is not required. Thus the question, "Your glasses were being repaired at the time of the accident, weren't they?" requires a good faith basis, while the question, "Were you wearing your glasses at the time of the accident?" does not.

1 Graham, Handbook of Federal Evidence § 607.2, at 679-80 (4th ed. 1996).

Using the term "reasonable basis," the amendment codifies the good-faith basis-in-fact requirement as recognized at common law. In addition to the Rules of Evidence, the Code of Professional Responsibility imposes requirements on questioning witnesses. See DR 7-106(C).

RULE 608. Evidence of Character and Conduct of Witness

(A)   Opinion and reputation evidence of character. The credibility of a witness may be attacked or supported by evidence in the form of opinion or reputation, but subject to these limitations: (1) the evidence may refer only to character for truthfulness or untruthfulness, and (2) evidence of truthful character is admissible only after the character of the witness for truthfulness has been attacked by opinion or reputation evidence or otherwise.

(B)   Specific instances of conduct. Specific instances of the conduct of a witness, for the purpose of attacking or supporting the witness's character for truthfulness, other than conviction of crime as provided in Evid. R. 609, may not be proved by extrinsic evidence. They may, however, in the discretion of the court, if clearly probative of truthfulness or untruthfulness, be inquired into on cross-examination of the witness (1) concerning the witness's character for truthfulness or untruthfulness, or (2) concerning the character for truthfulness or untruthfulness of another witness as to which character the witness being cross-examined has testified.

The giving of testimony by any witness, including an accused, does not operate as a waiver of the witness's privilege against self-incrimination when examined with respect to matters that relate only to the witness's character for truthfulness.

[Effective: July 1, 1980; July 1, 1992.]

Staff Note (July 1, 1992 Amendment)

Rule 608 Evidence of Character and Conduct of Witness
Rule 608(B) Specific instances of conduct

The amendment substitutes the phrase "character for truthfulness" for the term "credibility." The latter term is too broad and, therefore, may cause confusion.

Evid. R 608, along with Evid. R. 609 (prior convictions), concerns impeachment by means of character evidence. The rule does not deal with other methods of impeachment, such as bias, which is governed by Evid. R. 616, or prior inconsistent statements, which are governed by Evid. R. 613. Thus, the limitation on the admissibility of extrinsic evidence in Evid. R. 608(B) concerns only specific acts of conduct reflecting upon untruthful character, and not on "credibility" in general. Extrinsic evidence may be admissible under some other theory of impeachment. Indeed, Evid. R. 616 explicitly provides for the admissibility of extrinsic evidence of bias.

Extrinsic evidence of a prior inconsistent statement is admissible under Evid. R. 613(B), provided a foundation is laid on cross-examination. In addition, extrinsic evidence offered to show contradiction, an impeachment method not specifically covered by any rule, may be admissible under certain circumstances. *State v. Williams* (1984), 16 Ohio App.3d 484, 477 N.E. 2d 221 (testimony that rape complainant had engaged in sex with males in the course of prostitution admitted after complainant voluntarily testified that she had not consented to intercourse with defendant because she was a lesbian); G. Joseph & S. Saltzburg, Evidence in America: The Federal Rules in the States. ch. 42, at 9-10 (1987).

Commentators on the Federal Rules have recognized this problem. See A.B.A. Criminal Justice Section, *Federal Rules of Evidence: A Fresh Review and Evaluation*, 120 F.R.D. 299, 355 (1987) ("The root of the trouble seems to be the Rule's obscure wording. Perhaps foremost of the troubles .... is confusion concerning whether wrongdoing offered to show bias ...... rather than to show credibility-character, is covered by Rule 608(B).") The Federal Rules do not contain a rule on impeachment by bias. Nevertheless, the Supreme Court resolved the issue in *United States v. Abel* (1984), 469 U.S. 45, 105 S.Ct. 465, 83 L.Ed. 2d 450, holding extrinsic evidence of bias admissible notwithstanding Fed. R. Evid. 608(b).

See also La.Code Evid. art. 608(B) (phrase "character for truthfulness" used in lieu of "credibility").

In addition, masculine references are replaced by gender-neutral language, the style used for rule references is revised, and grammatical changes are made. No substantive change is intended.

RULE 609. Impeachment by Evidence of Conviction of Crime

(A) General rule. For the purpose of attacking the credibility of a witness:

(1) subject to Evid.R. 403, evidence that a witness other than the accused has been convicted of a crime is admissible if the crime was punishable by death or imprisonment in excess of one year pursuant to the law under which the witness was convicted.

(2) notwithstanding Evid.R. 403(A), but subject to Evid.R. 403(B), evidence that the accused has been convicted of a crime is admissible if the crime was punishable by death or imprisonment in excess of one year pursuant to the law under which the accused was convicted and if the court determines that the probative value of the evidence outweighs the danger of unfair prejudice, of confusion of the issues, or of misleading the jury.

(3) notwithstanding Evid.R. 403(A), but subject to Evid.R. 403(B), evidence that any witness, including an accused, has been convicted of a crime is admissible if the crime involved dishonesty or false statement, regardless of the punishment and whether based upon state or federal statute or local ordinance.

(B) Time limit. Evidence of a conviction under this rule is not admissible if a period of more than ten years has elapsed since the date of the conviction or of the release of the witness from the confinement, or the termination of community control sanctions, post-release control, or probation, shock probation, parole, or shock parole imposed for that conviction, whichever is the later date, unless the court determines, in the interests of justice, that the probative value of the conviction supported by specific facts and circumstances substantially outweighs its prejudicial effect. However, evidence of a conviction more than ten years old as calculated herein, is not admissible unless the proponent gives to the adverse party sufficient advance written notice of intent to use such evidence to provide the adverse party with a fair opportunity to contest the use of such evidence.

(C) Effect of pardon, annulment, expungement, or certificate of rehabilitation. Evidence of a conviction is not admissible under this rule if (1) the conviction has been the subject of a pardon, annulment, expungement, certificate of rehabilitation, or other equivalent procedure based on a finding of the rehabilitation of the person convicted, and that person has not been convicted of a subsequent crime which was punishable by death or imprisonment in excess of one year, or (2) the conviction has been the subject of a pardon, annulment, expungement, or other equivalent procedure based on a finding of innocence.

(D) Juvenile adjudications. Evidence of juvenile adjudications is not admissible except as provided by statute enacted by the General Assembly.

(E) Pendency of appeal. The pendency of an appeal therefrom does not render evidence of a conviction inadmissible. Evidence of the pendency of an appeal is admissible.

(F)   Methods of proof.   When evidence of a witness's conviction of a crime is admissible under this rule, the fact of the conviction may be proved only by the testimony of the witness on direct or cross-examination, or by public record shown to the witness during his or her examination. If the witness denies that he or she is the person to whom the public record refers, the court may permit the introduction of additional evidence tending to establish that the witness is or is not the person to whom the public record refers.

[Effective: July 1, 1980; amended effective July 1, 1991; July 1, 2003.]

Staff Note (July 1, 2003 amendment)

Rule 609   Impeachment by Evidence of Conviction of Crime

Rule 609(B)   Time limit

The amendment added references to "community control sanctions" and "post-release control" in division (B) to reflect the availability of those forms of sanction along with the traditional devices of probation and parole already referred to in the rule. Under the rule as amended, the termination of community control sanctions and post-release control become additional events from which to date the staleness of a conviction under the rule's presumptive exclusion of convictions that are remote in time.

Staff Note (July 1, 1991 Amendment)

Rule 609 Impeachment by Evidence of Conviction of Crime

The amendment makes several changes. One change concerns the trial court's discretion to exclude evidence of prior convictions, and the other change concerns permissible methods of proving prior convictions.

Rule 609(A) Discretion to exclude

The amended rule clarifies the issue of the trial court's discretion in excluding prior convictions. As adopted in 1980, the Ohio rule differed from its federal counterpart. A clause in Federal Rule 609(a)(1) explicitly authorized the trial court to exclude "felony" convictions; these convictions were admissible only if the "court determines that the probative value of admitting this evidence outweighs its prejudicial effect to the defendant." This clause was deleted from the Ohio rule.

It could have been argued that this deletion meant that Ohio courts did not have the authority to exclude prior felony convictions. In other words, any felony conviction was automatically admissible. Indeed, the rule specified that these convictions "shall be admitted." The Ohio Staff Note (1980), however, suggested otherwise. The Staff Note reads:

> In limiting that discretionary grant, Rule 609(A) is directed to greater uniformity in application subject only to the provisions of Rule 403. The removal of the reference to the defendant insures that the application of the rule is not limited to criminal prosecutions.

The Supreme Court addressed the issue in *State v. Wright* (1990), 48 Ohio St.3d 5, 548 N.E.2d 923. The Court wrote: "Evid. R. 609 must be considered in conjunction with Evid. R. 403. The trial judge therefore has broad discretion in determining the extent to which testimony will be admitted under Evid. R. 609."

The amended rule makes clear that Ohio trial judges have discretion to exclude prior convictions. It also specifies how this discretion is to be exercised. Evid. R. 609(A) is divided into three divisions.

Division (1) concerns "felony" convictions of witnesses other than the accused (prosecution and defense witnesses in criminal cases and all witnesses in civil cases). The admissibility of these convictions is subject to Evid. R. 403.

Division (A)(2) concerns "felony" convictions of an accused in a criminal case. The risk that a jury would misuse evidence of a prior conviction as evidence of propensity or general character, a use which is prohibited by Evid. R. 404, is far greater when a criminal accused is impeached. *See* C. McCormick, Evidence 99 (3d ed. 1984) ("The sharpest and most prejudicial impact of the practice of impeachment by conviction .... is upon .... the accused in a criminal case who elects to take the stand.")

Accordingly, admissibility of prior convictions is more readily achieved for witnesses other than the accused. Evid. R. 403 requires that the probative value of the evidence be "substantially" outweighed by unfair prejudice before exclusion is warranted. In other words, Evid. R. 403 is biased in favor of admissibility. This is not the case when the accused is impeached by a prior conviction under Evid. R. 609(A)(2); the unfair prejudice need only outweigh probative value, rather than "substantially" outweigh probative value.

In making this determination the court would consider a number of factors: "(1) the nature of the crime, (1) recency of the prior conviction, (3) similarity between the crime for which there was prior conviction and the crime charged, (4) the importance of defendant's testimony, and (5) the centrality of the credibility issue." C. McCormick, Evidence 94 n. 9 (3d ed. 1984).

Division (A)(3) concerns dishonesty and false statement convictions. Because of the high probative value of these convictions in assessing credibility, they are not subject to exclusion because of unfair prejudice. This rule applies to the accused as well as other witnesses.

The issue raised by Ohio Evid. R. 609 also is raised by the Federal Rule, even though the federal provision explicitly recognized trial judge discretion to exclude evidence of prior convictions. Because the discretionary language in the federal rule referred to balancing the prejudicial effect to the "defendant," the applicability of this clause to civil cases and prosecution witnesses had been questioned. The U.S. Supreme Court in *Green v. Bock Laundry* (1989), 490 U.S. 504, 109 S.Ct. 1981, 104 L.Ed. 2d 557, ruled that the discretion to exclude convictions under Federal Rule 609(a) did not apply to civil cases or to prosecution witnesses. Moreover, the court ruled that Rule 403 did not apply in this context. An amendment to the federal rule was adopted to change this result.

Rule 609(F) Methods of proof

The rule as adopted in 1980 specified that convictions admissible under the rule could be "elicited from him [the witness] or established by public record during cross-examination ..." The use of the term "cross-examination" was unfortunate. Custom permits counsel to bring out evidence of prior convictions on direct examination "for the purpose of lessening the import of these convictions upon the jury." *State v. Peoples* (1971), 28 Ohio Ap.2d 162, 168, 275 N.E.2d 626. Moreover, impeachment of a witness by proof of a prior conviction during direct examination is permitted under Evid. R. 607, which allows a party to impeach its own witnesses.

The traditional methods of proof are through examination of the witness or by public record. These methods are permissible under division (F).

RULE 610. Religious Beliefs or Opinions

Evidence of the beliefs or opinions of a witness on matters of religion is not admissible for the purpose of showing that by reason of their nature the witness' credibility is impaired or enhanced.

[Effective: July 1, 1980; amended effectively July 1, 2007.]

RULE 611. Mode and Order of Interrogation and Presentation

(A)   Control by court. The court shall exercise reasonable control over the mode and order of interrogating witnesses and presenting evidence so as to (1) make the interrogation and presentation effective for the ascertainment of the truth, (2) avoid needless consumption of time, and (3) protect witnesses from harassment or undue embarrassment.

(B)   Scope of cross-examination. Cross-examination shall be permitted on all relevant matters and matters affecting credibility.

(C)   Leading questions. Leading questions should not be used on the direct examination of a witness except as may be necessary to develop the witness' testimony. Ordinarily leading questions should be permitted on cross-examination. When a party calls a hostile witness, an adverse party, or a witness identified with an adverse party, interrogation may be by leading questions.

[Effective: July 1, 1980; amended effectively July 1, 2007.]

RULE 612.   Writing Used to Refresh Memory

If a witness uses a writing to refresh memory for the purpose of testifying, either: (1) while testifying; or (2) before testifying, if the court in its discretion determines it is necessary in the interests of justice, an adverse party is entitled to have the writing produced at the hearing. The adverse party is also entitled to inspect it, to cross-examine the witness thereon, and to introduce in evidence those portions which relate to the testimony of the witness. If it is claimed that the writing contains matters not related to the subject matter of the testimony the court shall examine the writing in camera, excise any portions not so related, and order delivery of the remainder to the party entitled thereto. Any portion withheld over objections shall be preserved and made available to the appellate court in the event of an appeal. If a writing is not produced or delivered pursuant to order under this rule, the court shall make any order justice requires, except that in criminal cases when the prosecution elects not to comply, the order shall be one striking the testimony or, if the court in its discretion determines that the interests of justice so require, declaring a mistrial.

[Effective: July 1, 1980; amended effectively July 1, 2007; July 1, 2011.]

RULE 613.   Impeachment by self-contradiction

(A)   Examining witness concerning prior statement.   In examining a witness concerning a prior statement made by the witness, whether written or not, the statement need not be shown nor its contents disclosed to the witness at that time, but on request the same shall be shown or disclosed to opposing counsel.

(B)   Extrinsic evidence of prior inconsistent statement of witness.   Extrinsic evidence of a prior inconsistent statement by a witness is admissible if both of the following apply:

(1)   If the statement is offered solely for the purpose of impeaching the witness, the witness is afforded a prior opportunity to explain or deny the statement and the opposite party is afforded an opportunity to interrogate the witness on the statement or the interests of justice otherwise require;

(2)   The subject matter of the statement is one of the following:

(a)   A fact that is of consequence to the determination of the action other than the credibility of a witness;

(b)   A fact that may be shown by extrinsic evidence under Evid.R. 608(A), 609, 616(A), or 616(B);

(c)   A fact that may be shown by extrinsic evidence under the common law of impeachment if not in conflict with the Rules of Evidence.

(C)   Prior inconsistent conduct.   During examination of a witness, conduct of the witness inconsistent with the witness's testimony may be shown to impeach. If offered for the sole purpose of impeaching the witness's testimony, extrinsic evidence of the prior inconsistent conduct is admissible under the same circumstances as provided for prior inconsistent statements by Evid.R. 613(B)(2).

[Effective: July 1, 1980; amended July 1, 1998; July 1, 2012.]

Staff Note (July 1, 1998 Amendment)

Rule 613 Impeachment by Self-Contradiction

The amendments codify aspects of the Ohio common law of impeachment concerning prior inconsistent statements and conduct. The title of the rule was changed from "Prior Statements of Witness" to "Impeachment by Self-Contradiction" to more accurately reflect the content of the rule, which deals with prior inconsistent conduct as well as prior inconsistent statements.

Rule 613(A) Examining witness concerning prior statement

Masculine references were made gender-neutral. There was no substantive amendment to this division.

Rule 613(B) Extrinsic evidence of prior inconsistent statement of witness

As adopted in 1980, Rule 613 did not fully specify the circumstances under which extrinsic evidence of a prior inconsistent statement is admissible. Division (B)(1) sets forth the foundational requirement for the admissibility of extrinsic evidence of prior inconsistent statements. There is no substantive change from the 1980 version of the rule. The introductory clause limits the rule to impeachment. Thus, statements that are admissible substantively, such as party admissions or excited utterances, are not governed by this rule, even though they may also have an impeaching effect.

Division (B)(2) sets forth three instances in which extrinsic evidence of a prior inconsistent statement is admissible. Division (B)(2)(a) permits extrinsic evidence if the subject matter of the prior statement is a consequential fact under the substantive law. See Evid.R. 401.

Extrinsic evidence is also admitted if the statement encompasses another method of impeachment that permits the introduction of extrinsic evidence, i.e., bias under Evid.R. 616(A), or the common law. These circumstances track those of impeachment by evidence of specific contradiction as provided in Rule 616(C). See Staff Note, Evid.R. 616(C) (1998).

Rule 613(C) Prior inconsistent conduct.

The 1998 amendment added division (C) to this rule. As adopted in 1980, Rule 613 did not provide for impeachment by evidence of prior inconsistent conduct. See Advisory Committee's Note, Fed. Evid.R. 613 ("Under principles of expression unius the rule does not apply to impeachment by evidence of prior inconsistent conduct."). Because no rule prohibits such impeachment, this type of evidence is admissible under Evid.R. 102 if relevant. See 1 McCormick, Evidence § 34, at 113 n. 5 (4th ed. 1992) ("Conduct . . . evincing a belief inconsistent with the facts asserted on the stand is usable on the same principle."). In a pre-Rules case, the Ohio Supreme Court wrote: "Conduct inconsistent with the testimony of a witness, may be shown as well as former statements thus inconsistent." *Dilcher v. State* (1883), 39 Ohio St. 130, 136 (1883). Accord *Westinghouse Electric Corp v. Dolly Madison Leasing & Furniture Corp.* (1975), 42 Ohio St.2d 122, 132, 326 N.E.2d 651 ("inconsistency in behavior" admissible for impeachment).

In *Westinghouse Electric Corp*, the Court imposed the same foundational requirements for impeachment by prior inconsistent conduct as were required for impeachment by prior inconsistent statements: "an adequate foundation for admission of the film was laid during cross-examination . . . and the witness was allowed to explain the apparent inconsistency upon redirect." 42 Ohio St.2d at 132.

This division applies only to the impeachment of a witness, including a party who testifies. It does not, however, apply to a party's inconsistent conduct that may be introduced on the merits; admissions by the conduct of a party (sometimes known as "implied admissions") may be admissible substantively and are not restricted by this rule. See 1 Giannelli & Snyder, Baldwin's Ohio Practice Evidence § 401.8-.10 (1996) (adverse inferences: spoliation, admissions by conduct, failure to produce evidence or call witnesses).

RULE 614.   Calling and Interrogation of Witnesses by Court

(A)   **Calling by court.** The court may, on its own motion or at the suggestion of a party, call witnesses, and all parties are entitled to cross-examine witnesses thus called.

(B)   **Interrogation by court.** The court may interrogate witnesses, in an impartial manner, whether called by itself or by a party.

(C)   **Objections.** Objections to the calling of witnesses by the court or to interrogation by it may be made at the time or at the next available opportunity when the jury is not present.

[Effective: July 1, 1980.]

RULE 615. Separation and Exclusion of Witnesses.

(A)   Except as provided in division (B) of this rule, at the request of a party the court shall order witnesses excluded so that they cannot hear the testimony of other witnesses, and it may make the order of its own motion. An order directing the "exclusion" or "separation" of witnesses or the like, in general terms without specification of other or additional limitations, is effective only to require the exclusion of witnesses from the hearing during the testimony of other witnesses.

(B)   This rule does not authorize exclusion of any of the following persons from the hearing:

(1)   a party who is a natural person;

(2)   an officer or employee of a party that is not a natural person designated as its representative by its attorney;

(3)   a person whose presence is shown by a party to be essential to the presentation of the party's cause;

(4)   in a criminal proceeding, a victim of the charged offense to the extent that the victim's presence is authorized by statute enacted by the General Assembly. As used in this rule, "victim" has the same meaning as in the provisions of the Ohio Constitution providing rights for victims of crimes.

[Effective: July 1, 1980; amended July 1, 2001; July 1, 2003.]

Staff Note (July 1, 2003 amendment)

Rule 615   Separation and Exclusion of Witnesses

The amendment changed the title of the rule from Exclusion of Witnesses to better reflect its subject matter, divided the rule into divisions to enhance clarity, and made a grammatical correction in new division (B)(2) (former division (B)). No substantive changes were intended by these modifications. Substantively, the amendment established requirements of specificity and notice for orders that regulate communications and contact by or with witnesses during a hearing.

Ohio courts have long exercised authority to order the "separation" of witnesses in order to limit the possibility that the witnesses' testimony might be influenced by the accounts of other witnesses. As originally adopted, Evid. R. 615 followed the federal model in addressing only one kind of separation order, that is, orders excluding witnesses from the courtroom during the testimony of other witnesses. Additional forms of separation were used in Ohio long before adoption of the rule, including, for example, orders limiting out-of-court contact between witnesses, or between witnesses and third-parties. Ohio courts have continued to employ these devices in the years since adoption of the rule. While the rule makes exclusion from the courtroom mandatory on the motion of a party, it is well established that trial courts continue to possess broad and flexible discretion in deciding what additional forms of separation, if any, are appropriate. The breadth of the discretion is reflected in the variety of different separation orders to be found in reported cases and in trial court practice. The variety of separation orders is accompanied by correspondingly diverse views among lawyers and courts (and sometimes among judges in the same court) regarding what additional forms of separation are generally appropriate or ought routinely to be imposed.

In practice, it is most common for trial courts to enter highly abbreviated orders on the subject. Normally a party will move for the "separation" (or "exclusion") of witnesses, and the court will respond with a general statement that the motion is granted. This is usually followed by an announcement to the gallery that prospective witnesses should leave the courtroom and by a statement that the parties are responsible for policing the presence of their own witnesses. Though some courts then orally announce additional limitations on communications to or by witnesses, the far more usual approach is simply to assume that the generic order of "separation" adequately conveys whatever limitations have been imposed.

The brevity of the rule and of most separation orders has led to "confusion about how far the scope of a bald Rule 615 order extends," *United States v. McMahon,* 104 F.3d 638, 648 (4th Cir.1997) (dissenting opinion). Some courts, in Ohio and elsewhere, have suggested that at least some additional forms of separation are implicit even in generally stated orders. This approach, however, entails significant issues of fair warning, since the "implicit" terms of an order may not be revealed to the parties or witnesses until after the putative violation has occurred. That is especially so when the "violation" involves conduct or communications about which there is a great diversity of opinion and practice. (Indeed, even among jurisdictions that follow this approach, there is disagreement as to what additional restrictions are necessarily implied in a generic separation order.) The imposition of sanctions without advance warning that the conduct is sanctionable raises obvious due-process concerns. Moreover, an "implicit-terms" approach is inconsistent with the principle that separation of witnesses beyond exclusion from the courtroom is neither automatic nor a matter of right: if witnesses and parties are bound by implicit additional restrictions whenever exclusion is ordered, then the additional restrictions are in fact automatic and non-discretionary.

The amendment rejects an "implicit-terms" approach and adopts instead the narrower rule employed by several Ohio courts and by what appears to be a majority of other jurisdictions that have addressed the question. Under this rule, generally-stated or "bald" separation orders are effective only to order the exclusion of witnesses from the courtroom during the testimony of other witnesses. *See, e.g., State v. Rogers* (Ohio App., 4th Distr., Nov. 15, 2000), unreported, 2000 WL 1728076, at *6-*7, *app. dism.* (2001), 91 Ohio St. 3d 1471. *See also U.S. v. Rhynes* (4th Cir. 2000), 218 F.3d 310, 321 n. 13 (en banc); *State v. Brown* (Conn. App. 1999), 741 A.2d 321, 325; *In re H.S.H.* (Ill. App. 2001), 751 N.E.2d 1236, 1241-1242. A separation order does not forbid other conduct by witnesses, such as being present during opening statements or discussing the case with other witnesses outside the courtroom. To the extent that a trial court, in the exercise of its discretion, determines to order forms of separation in addition to exclusion, it remains free to do so, but it can do so only by making the additional restrictions explicit and by giving the parties notice of the specific additional restrictions that have been ordered. Notice to the parties is required because, with the exception of contempt, sanctions for violation of the rule tend to have their greatest effect on the parties, rather on the witnesses.

The amendment does not define the standards for ordering forms of separation in addition to exclusion, or the kinds of additional separation that are permissible. Nor does the amendment address the matter of sanctions when a separation order has been violated. These subjects have long been committed to the sound discretion of trial courts to be exercised flexibly within well-established limits. *See, e.g., State v. Smith* (1990), 49 Ohio St.3d 137, 142 (excluding testimony as a sanction is proper only if the party calling the witness "consented to, connived in, [or] procured" the violation, or had knowledge of the witness's disobedience and failed to take affirmative steps to prevent it). The amendment does not change the law on these subjects.

Staff Note (July 1, 2001 Amendment)

Evidence Rule 615   Exclusion of Witnesses

Divisions (1) – (3) of the previous rule were redesignated as divisions (A) – (C). Clarifying punctuation was inserted immediately before division (A), and in division (C) a masculine reference was replaced with gender-neutral language. No substantive change was intended by either of these amendments.

The substantive amendment added division (D) to the rule recognizing a new category of witnesses who are not subject to an order excluding them from hearing the testimony of other witnesses. In particular, the amended rule permits the victim of an offense to be present at a criminal proceeding regarding the offense to the extent that the victim's presence is authorized by statute enacted by the General Assembly. The right of a victim to be present is limited to those persons who are "victims" within the meaning of the constitutional provisions regarding victims' rights. *See* Ohio Const., Art. I, § 10a. The amendment is designed to harmonize the rule with the provisions of R.C. 2930.09, which permits a victim to be present at any stage of a criminal proceeding conducted on the record (other than a grand jury proceeding) when the defendant is present, "unless the court determines that exclusion of the victim is necessary to protect the defendant's right to a fair trial."

Ordinarily, rules governing witness sequestration would be regarded as "procedural" matters within the meaning of the Modern Courts Amendment, Ohio Const., Art. IV, § 5(B), so that a rule of practice and procedure (such as Evid. R. 615) would prevail over an inconsistent statute on the same subject (such as R.C. 2930.09). In this instance, however, the statute involves an exercise of the General Assembly's power under the victims' rights provisions of the Ohio Constitution. Ohio Const., Art. I, § 10a. It is at least arguable that legislation enacted under the authority of section 10a is not displaced or rendered ineffective by reason of its inconsistency with a rule of practice and procedure. The amendment is intended to eliminate the conflict between the statute and the rule by deferring to the statutory right of a victim to be present at criminal proceedings. The deference extends only to the right of a *victim* to be present, and only in criminal proceedings. Moreover, whatever the statutory definition of "victim," the rule exempts from sequestration only those persons who are permitted by statute to be present *and* who are "victims" within the meaning of Article I, Section 10a of the Ohio Constitution. These limitations correspond to the extent of the General Assembly's power under the victims' rights provisions of the constitution.

The principal object of witness sequestration orders is to minimize the risk that a witness's testimony will be materially affected by hearing the testimony of other witnesses. Neither the statute nor the amended rule impairs the ability of trial courts to deal effectively with this risk when it exists. Under the statute (as well as under the constitution), the victim's right to be present is limited by the defendant's right to a fair trial. Thus, exclusion of a victim-witness would be permissible in cases in which the trial court is persuaded that the victim-witness's testimony would be altered by reason of the witness's presence during the testimony of other witnesses.

RULE 616. Methods of impeachment

In addition to other methods, a witness may be impeached by any of the following methods:

(A) Bias. Bias, prejudice, interest, or any motive to misrepresent may be shown to impeach the witness either by examination of the witness or by extrinsic evidence.

(B) Sensory or mental defect. A defect of capacity, ability, or opportunity to observe, remember, or relate may be shown to impeach the witness either by examination of the witness or by extrinsic evidence.

(C) Specific contradiction. Facts contradicting a witness's testimony may be shown for the purpose of impeaching the witness's testimony. If offered for the sole purpose of impeaching a witness's testimony, extrinsic evidence of contradiction is inadmissible unless the evidence is one of the following:

(1) Permitted by Evid.R. 608(A), 609, 613, 616(A), 616(B), or 706;

(2) Permitted by the common law of impeachment and not in conflict with the Rules of Evidence.

[Effective: July 1, 1991; amended July 1, 1998.]

Staff Note (July 1, 1998 Amendment)

Rule 616 Methods of Impeachment

The amendments to this rule codify two common law rules of impeachment, making them more readily accessible for trial use. The prior rule was lettered as division (A) but was not otherwise changed by the 1998 amendment; divisions (B) and (C) were added by this amendment. Also, the title of the rule was changed from "Bias of Witness" to "Methods of Impeachment."

Rule 616(B) Sensory or mental defect

The pre-Rules cases permitted inquiry into a witness's capacity to observe, remember, and recall. See *State v. Auerbach* (1923), 108 Ohio St. 96, 98, 140 N.E. 507 ("means of observation"); *Morgan v. State* (1891), 48 Ohio St. 371, 373-74, 27 N.E. 710 (opportunity to observe, "intelligence"); *Lee v. State* (1871), 21 Ohio St. 151, 154 (recollection), and *McAllister v. State* (App. 1932), 13 Ohio Abs. 360, 362 (mental condition affects credibility); as well as other factors affecting perception and memory. *Stewart v. State* (1850), 19 Ohio 302, 304 (proper to cross-examine witness on opportunity to observe and to remember).

The post-Rules cases are in accord. The Supreme Court has ruled that a witness's visual impairment is not a ground for incompetency under Evid.R. 601, but rather a factor "relat[ing] to the credibility of the statements made by [the witness]." *Turner v. Turner* (1993), 67 Ohio St.3d 337, 343, 617 N.E.2d 1123. See also *Kenney v. Fealko* (1991), 75 Ohio App.3d 47, 51, 598 N.E.2d 861 ("The Ohio Rules of Evidence do not enumerate the various ways in which the credibility of a witness can properly be attacked. . . . Under [Evid.R. 611(B)] and the common-law rule, evidence of appellant's state of intoxication was admissible because it was relevant to the issue of her ability to perceive and hence her credibility.").

Division (B) provides for the admissibility of this type of evidence on cross-examination or through extrinsic evidence (i.e., the testimony of other witnesses). This provision does not change Evid. R. 601, which governs the competency of witnesses, or Evid. R. 602, which specifies the firsthand-knowledge requirement. The admissibility of expert testimony on these issues must satisfy the requirement of Rule 702.

Rule 616(C) Specific contradiction

There are two distinct methods of impeachment by contradiction. First, self-contradiction involves the use of a witness's own prior inconsistent statements or conduct to contradict the witness's present testimony. Evid. R. 613 governs this type of impeachment.

Second, contradiction may involve the testimony of one witness that conflicts with the testimony of another witness (called "specific contradiction"). The circumstances under which a party may introduce extrinsic evidence of contradiction is typically stated in terms of the so-called "collateral matters" rule. E.g., *Byomin v. Alvis* (1959), 169 Ohio St. 395, 396, 159 N.E.2d 897 (per curiam) ("It is elementary that a witness may not be impeached by evidence that merely contradicts his testimony on a matter that is collateral."); *State v. Cochrane* (1949), 151 Ohio St. 128, 135, 84 N.E.2d 742 ("The cross-examiner is not permitted to introduce rebuttal evidence to contradict the witness on collateral matters.").

The common law rule does not prohibit a party from cross-examining on a "collateral matter." It prohibits only the introduction of extrinsic evidence on the issue. The policy underlying this rule is to "avoid[] the dangers of surprise, jury confusion and wasted time which are the reasons for the rule against impeachment on collateral matters." *State v. Kehn* (1977), 50 Ohio St.2d 11, 17, 361 N.E.2d 1330 (per curiam), cert. denied, 434 U.S. 858, 98 S.Ct. 180, 54 L.Ed.2d 130 (1977).

According to Wigmore, extrinsic evidence of contradiction should be admitted if the evidence would be admissible "for any purpose independently of the contradiction." 3A Wigmore, Evidence § 1003, at 961 (Chadbourn rev. 1970). Explaining this test,

McCormick wrote that two types of facts were independently provable: "The first kind are facts that are relevant to the substantive issues in the case". McCormick, Evidence § 47, at 110-11 (3d ed. 1984). Because Rule 616(C) is limited to impeachment, evidence concerning the substantive issues is governed by Rules 401 to 403, not this rule.

The second category are "facts showing bias, interest, conviction of crime, and want of capacity or opportunity for knowledge." Id. In other words, the second category encompasses those methods of impeachment, such as bias, that always permit the introduction of extrinsic evidence. The Ohio Supreme Court appears to have adopted Wigmore's approach in an early case. *Kent v. State* (1884), 42 Ohio St. 426, 431 (Extrinsic evidence is admissible when "the matter offered in contradiction is in any way relevant to the issue, or such as tends to show prejudice or interest."). Evid. R. 616(C)(1) enumerates the rules that fall within this category.

McCormick argued that extrinsic evidence of contradiction should also be admitted in a third situation, one in which such evidence is critical to determining the credibility of a witness's story. He refers to this as "linchpin" evidence: "So we may recognize this third type of allowable contradiction, namely, the contradiction of any part of the witness's account of the background and circumstances of a material transaction, which as a matter of human experience he would not have been mistaken about if his story was true." McCormick, Evidence § 47, at 112 (3d ed. 1984). McCormick provides several examples: *Stephens v. People,* 19 N.Y. 549, 572 (1859) (murder by poisoning with arsenic; defendant's witnesses testified the arsenic was administered to rats in cellar where provisions kept; held proper for state to prove by another witness that no provisions were kept in cellar); *Hartsfield v. Carolina Cas. Ins. Co.,* 451 P.2d 576 (Alaska 1969) (on issue whether insurance cancellation notice was sent to defendant by insurer, defendant denied receipt and also receipt of notices of cancellations of the insurance from two other sources. Evidence of the mailing by the two latter sources was held not collateral). Division (C)(2) of this rule encompasses this category. The phrase "not in conflict with these rules" is intended to ensure that this provision is not used to circumvent the prohibition on the admissibility of extrinsic evidence of specific acts found in Evid. R. 608(B); Evid. R. 608(B) controls.

In the impeachment context, extrinsic evidence means evidence introduced through the testimony of other witnesses. See 1 McCormick, Evidence § 36, at 118 (4th ed. 1992) ("Extrinsic evidence, that is, the production of attacking witnesses . . . is sharply narrowed for obvious reasons of economy of time and attention."). Accordingly, documentary evidence offered through the witness being impeached is not extrinsic evidence because it typically does not consume much additional time.

Staff Note (July 1, 1991 Amendment)

Rule 616 Methods of impeachment

As originally adopted, neither the Ohio nor the Federal Rules contained a rule governing impeachment regarding bias or interest. In *United States v. Abel* (1984), 469 U.S. 45, 105 S.Ct. 465, 83 L.Ed. 2d 450, the U.S. Supreme Court held that impeachment of a witness for bias was proper, notwithstanding the lack of a specific rule. According to the Court, "the lesson to be drawn . . . . is that it is permissible to impeach a witness by showing his bias under the Fed. Rules of Evid. just as it was permissible to do before their adoption." *Id.* at 51.

Impeachment by bias also is permitted in Ohio. R.C. 2945.42 provides: "No person is disqualified as a witness in a criminal prosecution by reason of his interest in the prosecution as a party or otherwise. . . . .Such interest . . . . may be shown for the purpose of affecting the credibility of such witness." In addition, the Ohio Supreme Court has written: "It is beyond question that a witness' bias and prejudice by virtue of pecuniary interest in the outcome of the proceeding is a matter affecting credibility under Evid. R. 611(B)." *State v. Ferguson* (1983), 5 Ohio St.3d 160, 165, 450 N.E.2d 265. Evid. R. 611(B), however, is the general provision on cross-examination and does not mention explicitly the term bias.

The Rules of Evidence contain a number of impeachment rules (Rules 607, 608, 609, and 613). Because of its importance as a traditional method of impeachment, bias also should be explicitly treated in the Rules of Evidence, as it is in some jurisdictions. *See* Unif. R. Evid. 616; Haw. R. Evid. 609.1; Utah R. Evid. 608(c); Mil. R. Evid. 608(c).

ARTICLE VII. OPINIONS AND EXPERT TESTIMONY

RULE 701.   Opinion Testimony by Lay Witnesses

If the witness is not testifying as an expert, the witness' testimony in the form of opinions or inferences is limited to those opinions or inferences which are (1) rationally based on the perception of the witness and (2) helpful to a clear understanding of the witness' testimony or the determination of a fact in issue.

[Effective: July 1, 1980; amended effectively July 1, 2007.]

RULE 702. Testimony by Experts

A witness may testify as an expert if all of the following apply:

(A) The witness' testimony either relates to matters beyond the knowledge or experience possessed by lay persons or dispels a misconception common among lay persons;

(B) The witness is qualified as an expert by specialized knowledge, skill, experience, training, or education regarding the subject matter of the testimony;

(C) The witness' testimony is based on reliable scientific, technical, or other specialized information. To the extent that the testimony reports the result of a procedure, test, or experiment, the testimony is reliable only if all of the following apply:

(1) The theory upon which the procedure, test, or experiment is based is objectively verifiable or is validly derived from widely accepted knowledge, facts, or principles;

(2) The design of the procedure, test, or experiment reliably implements the theory;

(3) The particular procedure, test, or experiment was conducted in a way that will yield an accurate result.

[Effective: July 1, 1980; amended effective July 1, 1994.]

Staff Note (July 1, 1994 Amendment)

Rule 702 Testimony by Experts

The amendment is intended to clarify the circumstances in which expert testimony is admissible, a subject on which the language of the pre-amendment rule has proved to be uninformative and, at times, misleading. Because the intention is to reflect the Ohio Supreme Court's interpretations of the rule's pre-amendment language, no substantive change from prior law is intended. In particular, there is no intention to change existing Ohio law regarding the reliability of expert testimony.

As originally adopted, Evid. R. 702 employed the same language as is used in the Federal Rules of Evidence to define the admissibility of expert testimony. That language permits a witness with the appropriate expertise to testify as an expert if the testimony "will assist the trier of fact." Evid. R. 702 (1980); F.R. Evid., Rule 702.

The "assist the trier" standard has been the subject of widely varying interpretations in the jurisdictions that have adopted it. In Ohio, however, decisions by the Supreme Court have established that the phrase incorporates two distinct admissibility requirements in addition tot the witness's expertise.

First, as at common law, an expert's testimony "assist[s] the trier" only if it relates to a matter "beyond the ken" of the ordinary person. *State v. Koss* (1990), 49 Ohio St. 3d 213, 216 (expert testimony is not admissible "when such knowledge is within the ken of the jury"); *State v. Buell* (1980)k, 22 Ohio St. 3d 124, 131 (expert testimony is admissible if the subject is "sufficiently beyond common experience), cert denied, 479 U.S. 871 (1986); *State v. Thomas* (1981), 66 Ohio St. 2d 518, 521 (expert testimony is inadmissible if the subject is not "beyond the ken of the average lay person").

Second, the expert's testimony "Assist[s] the trier" only if it meets a threshold standard of reliability, as established either by testimony or by judicial notice. (The trier of fact remains free, of course to make its own assessment of reliability and to accept or reject the testimony accordingly once it has been admitted.) See *State v. Bresson* (1990), 51 Ohio St. 3d 123, 128 (prior case-law establishing reliability of test sufficed to show reliability as a general matter, and test was admissible on a case-specific showing regarding the tester's qualifications and the reliability of the specific test administration); *State v. Williams* (1983), 4 Ohio St. 3d 53, 59 (expert testimony as to test was admissible "[I]n view of the unrebutted evidence of reliability of [the test] in general, and of [the witness's] analysis in particular"). See also *State v. Pierce* (1992), 64 Ohio St. 3d 490, 494-501 (scientific evidence was admissible where unreliability in specific case was not shown and where balance of probative value and reliability against risk of misleading or confusing the jury did not warrant exclusion).

As to the reliability requirement, the Ohio cases have not adopted a definitive test of the showing required for expert testimony generally. The Ohio cases have, however, clearly rejected the standard of *Frye v. United States* (D.C. Cir. 1923), 293 F. 1013, under which scientific opinions are admissible only if the theory or test in question enjoys "general acceptance" within a relevant scientific community. See *Williams, supra*, 4 Ohio St. 3d at 58; *Pierce, supra*, 64 Ohio St. 3d at 496. See also *Daubert v. Merrell Dow Pharmaceuticals, Inc.* (1993, ____ U.S. ____, 113 S. Ct. 2786 (similarly rejecting *Frye* and describing the reliability standard to be employed under the federal counterpart to Evid. R. 702.)

Under Ohio law it is also clear that reliability is properly determined only by reference to the principles and methods employed by the expert witness, without regard to whether the court regards the witness's conclusions themselves as persuasive or correct. See *Pierce, supra*, 64 Ohio St. 3d at 498 (emphasizing that unreliability could not be shown by differences in the conclusions of experts, without evidence that the procedures employed were "somehow deficient"). See also *Daubert, supra*, 113 S.Ct. at 2797 (the focus "must be solely on principles and methodology, not on the conclusions they generate").

In view of the interpretation given to the "assist the trier" standard by the Ohio Supreme Court's decisions, the rule's original language has been at best uninformative, and it appears to have been affirmatively misleading in some cases. It has been unhelpful to courts and attorneys seeking guidance on the admissibility of challenged testimony, often in the midst of trial, because the language itself does not self-evidently convey the specific content that has been given to it by authoritative judicial interpretations.

Moreover, a review of intermediate appellate decisions suggests that the language has been misleading to at least some Ohio lawyers and courts. In particular, in some cases, the parties and the courts have relied on decisions from other jurisdictions that have given a different content to the phrase "assist the trier," and they have as a result mistakenly assumed that Ohio law is in accord with the law of those other jurisdictions.

The amendment is intended to enhance the utility of the rule, and to reduce the occasions for mistaken interpretation, by substituting a codification of the above-noted Supreme Court holdings in place of the vague and misleading "assist the trier" language. Thus, the amended rule expressly states the three existing requirements for the admissibility of expert testimony:

(1) The witness must be qualified to testify by reason of specialized knowledge, skill, experience, training, or education. Evid. R. 702(B), incorporating original Evid. R. 702.

(2) the witness's testimony must relate to matters beyond the knowledge or experience possessed by lay persons, or dispel a misconception common among lay persons. Evid. R. 702(A), codifying *Koss, Buell*, and *Thomas, supra*. (The reference to "dispel[ling] a misconception" is a codification of the specific holding in *Koss, supra*, 49 Ohio St. 3d at 216, that the permissible subject matter of expert testimony includes not only matters beyond common knowledge, but also matters of common but mistaken belief.)

(3)   The witness's testimony must have its basis in reliable scientific, technical, or otherwise specialized knowledge. Evid. R. 702(C), codifying *Bresson* and *Williams*, *supra*. As to evidence regarding a "test, procedure, or experiment," reliability must be shown both as to the test generally (that is, the underlying theory and the implementation of the theory), Evid. R. 702(C)(1) and (2), and as to the specific application. Evid. R. 702(C)(3). See *Bresson, supra*; *Williams, supra*. See generally 1 P. Giannelli and E. Imwinkelried, Scientific Evidence 1-2 (2d ed. 1993).

Consistent with the intention to do no more than codify existing holdings on the admissibility of expert testimony, the amended rule does not attempt to define the standard of reliability but leaves that to further development through case law. The amendment also leaves unchanged Ohio's rejection of *Frye* as the exclusive standard of reliability. Similarly, the amendment does not purport to supplant existing case law as to the acceptable means for showing reliability, whether through judicial notice or testimony. Further, the law remains unchanged that the inquiry as to reliability is appropriately directed, not to the correctness or credibility of the conclusions reached by the expert witness, but to the reliability of the principles and methods used to reach those conclusions.

(While decisions under the federal rules of evidence are frequently inapposite to the interpretation of the Ohio rules, see Evid. R. 102, the federal counterpart to Evid. R. 702 has been interpreted as incorporating a reliability requirement. *Daubert, supra*. To that extent, the United States Supreme Court's discussion of the considerations that may be relevant to a reliability determination may also be helpful in construing the Ohio rule. See id., 113 S. Ct. at 2795-2796.)

Because the amendment is not intended to change existing law, the procedure for challenging and determining the admissibility of expert proofs likewise remains unchanged. As has been true under the original rule, there may be cases where the issues raised by a proffer of expert testimony can be most efficiently resolved by pre-trial hearing, briefing, and argument. In other cases, however, the issues can be resolved as adequately by objection and decision during trial. In either case, these have been, and will continue to be, matters that are determined by the timing of the parties' motions and by the scheduling and supervisory authority of the trial court.

RULE 703.   Bases of Opinion Testimony by Experts

The facts or data in the particular case upon which an expert bases an opinion or inference may be those perceived by the expert or admitted in evidence at the hearing.

[Effective: July 1, 1980; amended effectively July 1, 2007.]

RULE 704.   Opinion on Ultimate Issue

Testimony in the form of an opinion or inference otherwise admissible is not objectionable solely because it embraces an ultimate issue to be decided by the trier of fact.

[Effective: July 1, 1980.]

RULE 705.   Disclosure of Facts or Data Underlying Expert Opinion

The expert may testify in terms of opinion or inference and give the expert's reasons therefor after disclosure of the underlying facts or data. The disclosure may be in response to a hypothetical question or otherwise.

[Effective: July 1, 1980; amended effectively July 1, 2007.]

Staff Note (July 1, 2006 Amendment)

Rule 706 Learned Treatises for Impeachment

Evid. R. 706 is repealed, effective July 1, 2006, in light of the adoption of Evid. R. 803(18).

Staff Note (July 1, 1998 Amendment)

Rule 706 Learned Treatises for Impeachment.

The common law rule restricted the use of a learned treatise to impeachment. See *Hallworth v. Republic Steel Corp.*, (1950) 153 Ohio St. 349, 91 N.E.2d 690 (syllabus, para. 2) ("Medical books or treatises, even though properly identified and authenticated and shown to be recognized as standard authorities on the subject to which they relate, are not admissible in evidence to prove the truth of the statements therein contained."). When the Rules of Evidence were adopted in 1980, Ohio rejected Federal Evidence Rule 803(18), which recognizes a hearsay exception for learned treatises. Consequently, the common law impeachment rule continued, under Evid. R. 102, as the controlling precedent in Ohio. See *Ramage v. Cent. Ohio Emergency Serv. Inc.* (1992), 64 Ohio St.3d. 87, 110, 592 N.E.2d 828 ("In Ohio, textbooks and other learned treatises are considered hearsay, may not be used as substantive evidence, and are specially limited to impeachment purposes only.").

This new Rule of Evidence codifies the common law rule, making it more readily accessible for trial use. The syllabus in *Hallworth* referred to treatises "recognized as standard authorities," without requiring reliance by the expert. In a post-Rules case, the Supreme Court wrote: "[I]n Ohio, a learned treatise may be used for impeachment purposes to demonstrate that an expert witness is either unaware of the text or unfamiliar with its contents. Moreover, the substance of the treatise may be employed only to impeach the credibility of an expert who has relied upon the treatise, . . ., or has acknowledged its authoritative nature." *Stinson v. England* (1994), 69 Ohio St.3d 451, 458, 633 N.E.2d 532.

A possible expansion of the common law rule concerns the use of judicial notice to establish the treatise as a reliable authority. A court taking judicial notice of Gray's Anatomy illustrates this aspect of the rule.

The trial court decides under Evid. R. 104(A) if the treatise is a "reliable authority" and Evid. R. 105 requires a limiting instruction upon request. If an opposing expert witness refuses to recognize a treatise as reliable, the judge may permit the impeachment subject to counsel's subsequent laying of the foundation through its own expert. There is no need to inform the jury of the trial court's determination.

ARTICLE VIII. HEARSAY

RULE 801. Definitions

The following definitions apply under this article:

(A) Statement. A "statement" is (1) an oral or written assertion or (2) nonverbal conduct of a person, if it is intended by the person as an assertion.

(B) Declarant. A "declarant" is a person who makes a statement.

(C) Hearsay. "Hearsay" is a statement, other than one made by the declarant while testifying at the trial or hearing, offered in evidence to prove the truth of the matter asserted.

(D) Statements which are not hearsay. A statement is not hearsay if:

(1) Prior statement by witness. The declarant testifies at trial or hearing and is subject to cross-examination concerning the statement, and the statement is (a) inconsistent with declarant's testimony, and was given under oath subject to cross-examination by the party against whom the statement is offered and subject to the penalty of perjury at a trial, hearing, or other proceeding, or in a deposition, or (b) consistent with declarant's testimony and is offered to rebut an express or implied charge against declarant of recent fabrication or improper influence or motive, or (c) one of identification of a person soon after perceiving the person, if the circumstances demonstrate the reliability of the prior identification.

(2) Admission by party-opponent. The statement is offered against a party and is (a) the party's own statement, in either an individual or a representative capacity, or (b) a statement of which the party has manifested an adoption or belief in its truth, or (c) a statement by a person authorized by the party to make a statement concerning the subject, or (d) a statement by the party's agent or servant concerning a matter within the scope of the agency or employment, made during the existence of the relationship, or (e) a statement by a co-conspirator of a party during the course and in furtherance of the conspiracy upon independent proof of the conspiracy.

[Effective: July 1, 1980; amended effectively July 1, 2007.]

RULE 802.   Hearsay Rule

Hearsay is not admissible except as otherwise provided by the Constitution of the United States, by the Constitution of the State of Ohio, by statute enacted by the General Assembly not in conflict with a rule of the Supreme Court of Ohio, by these rules, or by other rules prescribed by the Supreme Court of Ohio.

[Effective: July 1, 1980.]

RULE 803.   Hearsay Exceptions; Availability of Declarant Immaterial

The following are not excluded by the hearsay rule, even though the declarant is available as a witness:

(1)   Present sense impression. A statement describing or explaining an event or condition made while the declarant was perceiving the event or condition, or immediately thereafter unless circumstances indicate lack of trustworthiness.

(2)   Excited utterance. A statement relating to a startling event or condition made while the declarant was under the stress of excitement caused by the event or condition.

(3)   Then existing, mental, emotional, or physical condition. A statement of the declarant's then existing state of mind, emotion, sensation, or physical condition (such as intent, plan, motive, design, mental feeling, pain, and bodily health), but not including a statement of memory or belief to prove the fact remembered or believed unless it relates to the execution, revocation, identification, or terms of declarant's will.

(4)   Statements for purposes of medical diagnosis or treatment. Statements made for purposes of medical diagnosis or treatment and describing medical history, or past or present symptoms, pain, or sensations, or the inception or general character of the cause or external source thereof insofar as reasonably pertinent to diagnosis or treatment.

(5)   Recorded recollection. A memorandum or record concerning a matter about which a witness once had knowledge but now has insufficient recollection to enable him to testify fully and accurately, shown by the testimony of the witness to have been made or adopted when the matter was fresh in his memory and to reflect that knowledge correctly. If admitted, the memorandum or record may be read into evidence but may not itself be received as an exhibit unless offered by an adverse party.

(6)   Records of regularly conducted activity. A memorandum, report, record, or data compilation, in any form, of acts, events, or conditions, made at or near the time by, or from information transmitted by, a person with knowledge, if kept in the course of a regularly conducted business activity, and if it was the regular practice of that business activity to make the memorandum, report, record, or data compilation, all as shown by the testimony of the custodian or other qualified witness or as provided by Rule 901(B)(10), unless the source of information or the method or circumstances of preparation indicate lack of trustworthiness. The term "business" as used in this paragraph includes business, institution, association, profession, occupation, and calling of every kind, whether or not conducted for profit.

(7)   Absence of entry in record kept in accordance with the provisions of paragraph (6). Evidence that a matter is not included in the memoranda, reports, records, or data compilations, in any form, kept in accordance with the provisions of paragraph (6), to prove the nonoccurrence or nonexistence of the matter, if the matter was of a kind of which a memorandum, report, record, or data compilation was regularly made and preserved, unless the sources of information or other circumstances indicate lack of trustworthiness.

(8)   Public records and reports. Records, reports, statements, or data compilations, in any form, of public offices or agencies, setting forth (a) the activities of the office or agency, or (b) matters observed pursuant to duty imposed by law as to which matters there was a duty to report, excluding, however, in criminal cases matters observed by police officers and other law enforcement personnel, unless offered by defendant, unless the sources of information or other circumstances indicate lack of trustworthiness.

(9)   Records of vital statistics. Records or data compilations, in any form, of births, fetal deaths, deaths, or marriages, if the report thereof was made to a public office pursuant to requirement of law

(10)   Absence of public record. Testimony—or a certification under Evid.R. 901(B)(10)—that a diligent search failed to disclose a public record or statement if:

(a)   the testimony or certification is admitted to prove that

(i)   the record or statement does not exist; or

(ii)   a matter did not occur or exist, if a public office regularly kept a record or statement for a matter of that kind; and

(b)   in a criminal case, a prosecutor who intends to offer a certification provides written notice of that intent at least 14 days before trial, and the defendant does not object in writing within 7 days of receiving the notice — unless the court sets a different time for the notice or the objection.

(11)   Records of religious organizations. Statements of births, marriages, divorces, deaths, legitimacy, ancestry, relationship by blood or marriage, or other similar facts of personal or family history, contained in a regularly kept record of a religious organization.

(12)   Marriage, baptismal, and similar certificates. Statements of fact contained in a certificate that the maker performed a marriage or other ceremony or administered a sacrament, made by a clergyman, public official, or other person authorized by the rules or practices of a religious organization or by law to perform the act certified, and purporting to have been issued at the time of the act or within a reasonable time thereafter.

(13)   Family records. Statements of fact concerning personal or family history contained in family Bibles, genealogies, charts, engravings on rings, inscriptions on family portraits, engravings on urns, crypts, or tombstones, or the like.

(14) **Records of documents affecting an interest in property.** The record of a document purporting to establish or affect an interest in property, as proof of the content of the original recorded document and its execution and delivery by each person by whom it purports to have been executed, if the record is a record of a public office and an applicable statute authorizes the recording of documents of that kind in that office.

(15) **Statements in documents affecting an interest in property.** A statement contained in a document purporting to establish or affect an interest in property if the matter stated was relevant to the purpose of the document, unless dealings with the property since the document was made have been inconsistent with the truth of the statement or the purport of the document.

(16) **Statements in ancient documents.** Statements in a document in existence twenty years or more the authenticity of which is established.

(17) **Market reports, commercial publications.** Market quotations, tabulations, lists, directories, or other published compilations, generally used and relied upon by the public or by persons in particular occupations.

(18) **Learned Treatises.** To the extent called to the attention of an expert witness upon cross-examination or relied upon by the expert witness in direct examination, statements contained in published treatises, periodicals, or pamphlets on a subject of history, medicine, or other science or art, established as a reliable authority by the testimony or admission of the witness or by other expert testimony or by judicial notice. If admitted, the statements may be read into evidence but may not be received as exhibits.

(19) **Reputation concerning personal or family history.** Reputation among members of the declarant's family by blood, adoption, or marriage or among the declarant's associates, or in the community, concerning a person's birth, adoption, marriage, divorce, death, legitimacy, relationship by blood, adoption or marriage, ancestry, or other similar fact of the declarant's personal or family history.

(20) **Reputation concerning boundaries or general history.** Reputation in a community, arising before the controversy, as to boundaries of or customs affecting lands in the community, and reputation as to events of general history important to the community or state or nation in which located.

(21) **Reputation as to character.** Reputation of a person's character among the person's associates or in the community.

(22) **Judgment of previous conviction.** Evidence of a final judgment, entered after a trial or upon a plea of guilty (but not upon a plea of no contest or the equivalent plea from another jurisdiction), adjudging a person guilty of a crime punishable by death or imprisonment in excess of one year, to prove any fact essential to sustain the judgment, but not including, when offered by the Government in a criminal prosecution for purposes other than impeachment, judgments against persons other than the accused. The pendency of an appeal may be shown but does not affect admissibility.

(23) **Judgment as to personal, family, or general history, or boundaries.** Judgments as proof of matters of personal, family or general history, or boundaries, essential to the judgment, if the same would be provable by evidence of reputation.

[Effective: July 1, 1980; amended effective July 1, 2006; July 1, 2007; July 1, 2016.]

Staff Note (July 1, 2006 Amendment)

The 2006 amendment adds a new hearsay exception for statements in reliable learned treatises that are relied on by expert witnesses on direct examination or are called to the attention of expert witnesses on cross-examination. The 2006 amendment also renumbers five existing hearsay exceptions to reflect the insertion of Evid. R. 803(18).

Evid. R. 706, adopted in 1998, is repealed in view of the adoption of Evid. R. 803(18).

Rule 803(18) Learned Treatises

Evid. R. 803(18) is modeled on Federal Rule of Evidence 803(18), which has been described as a "carefully drafted rule [that] appears to work well in practice." Robert F. Magill, Jr., *Issues Under Federal Rule of Evidence 803(18): The "Learned Treatise" Exception to the Hearsay Rule,* 9 St. John's J. Legal Comment. 49 (1993). Although a departure from the common law and Ohio practice, substantive use of learned treatises is now accepted by the majority of states, Clifford Fishman, Jones on Evidence 316 (7th ed., 2003).

There are a number of reasons for creating a hearsay exception for statements in learned treatises under the circumstances in the proposed rule. Every expert brings a certain amount of "background hearsay" to his or her opinion, in the form of the out-of-court statements of textbook authors, colleagues, and others, that forms much of the basis of the expert's training and education. Paul Gianelli, Understanding Evidence 347 (2003). Ohio law now allows experts to rely on that knowledge in establishing their qualifications and in forming opinions. *Worthington City Schools v. ABCO Insulation,* 84 Ohio App. 3d 144, 152 (1992); *State v. Echols,* 128 Ohio App. 3d 677, 698 (Ham.1998). The rule makes explicit the sources of the expert's opinion, and in doing so both avoids disputes about the level of detail in their testimony and assists the trier of fact in evaluating that testimony. *Beard v. Meridia Huron Hosp.,* 106 Ohio St.3d 237, 2005-Ohio-4787. Similarly, while former law permitted the use of learned treatises for impeachment on cross-examination, Ohio Rule of Evidence 706, and on redirect examination after impeachment, *Hinkle v. Cleveland Clinic Foundation,* 159 Ohio App. 3d. 351, 365 (Cuy. 2004), it is often difficult for a jury to understand or maintain the distinction between impeachment or rehabilitation, on the one hand, and substantive use on the other.

Importantly, commentators agree that statements in learned treatises come within the two major justifications for most hearsay exceptions: reliability and necessity. David H. Kaye, *et. al.,* The New Wigmore: A Treatise on Evidence: Expert Evidence 132 (2004). Authors of scholarly works usually have no connection to the litigation and no motive to misrepresent. Their scholarly reputations are at stake when peers review their work for accuracy, enhancing reliability. With respect to necessity, there is often no other way to get the opinions of the most highly qualified researchers and scholars before the court.

Evid. R. 803(18) contains a number of safeguards against unreliability and misuse. Misunderstanding is guarded against by the fact that the statements in learned treatises come to the trier of fact only through the testimony of qualified experts who are on the stand to explain and apply the material in the treatise. The rule provides that the treatise may be read into evidence but not received as an exhibit to prevent the trier from giving it excessive weight or attempting to interpret the treatise by itself. The rule applies only to a learned treatise found by the judge to be a "reliable authority" under Evid. R. 104(A).

Staff Note (July 1, 2016 Amendment)

The amendment adopts the 2011 federal stylistic changes made to the introductory language of Fed.R.Evid. 803 and to Fed.R.Evid. 803(10).

The amendment also adds Evid.R. 803(10)(b) which is modeled on a similar amendment made to Fed.R.Evid. 803(10) in 2013 in response to the United States Supreme Court ruling in *Melendez-Diaz v. Massachusetts*, 557. U.S. 305 (2009). As explained in the Federal Advisory Committee notes to the 2013 amendment, the *Melendez-Diaz* Court declared that a testimonial certificate could be admitted if the accused is given advance notice and does not timely demand the presence of the official who prepared the certificate. The language of Fed.R.Evid. 803(10)(B) and Ohio Evid.R. 803(10)(b) incorporates, with minor variations, a "notice-and-demand" procedure that was approved by the *Melendez-Diaz* Court.

RULE 804.   Hearsay Exceptions; Declarant Unavailable

RULE 804   **Hearsay Exceptions; Declarant Unavailable**

(A)   Definition of unavailability. "Unavailability as a witness" includes any of the following situations in which the declarant:

(1)   is exempted by ruling of the court on the ground of privilege from testifying concerning the subject matter of the declarant's statement;

(2)   persists in refusing to testify concerning the subject matter of the declarant's statement despite an order of the court to do so;

(3)   testifies to a lack of memory of the subject matter of the declarant's statement;

(4)   is unable to be present or to testify at the hearing because of death or then-existing physical or mental illness or infirmity;

(5)   is absent from the hearing and the proponent of the declarant's statement has been unable to procure the declarant's attendance (or in the case of a hearsay exception under division (B)(2), (3), or (4) of this rule, the declarant's attendance or testimony) by process or other reasonable means.

A declarant is not unavailable as a witness if the declarant's exemption, refusal, claim of lack of memory, inability, or absence is due to the procurement or wrongdoing of the proponent of the declarant's statement for the purpose of preventing the witness from attending or testifying.

(B)   Hearsay exceptions. The following are not excluded by the hearsay rule if the declarant is unavailable as a witness:

(1)   Former testimony. Testimony given as a witness at another hearing of the same or a different proceeding, or in a deposition taken in compliance with law in the course of the same or another proceeding, if the party against whom the testimony is now offered, or, in a civil action or proceeding, a predecessor in interest, had an opportunity and similar motive to develop the testimony by direct, cross, or redirect examination. Testimony given at a preliminary hearing must satisfy the right to confrontation and exhibit indicia of reliability.

(2)   Statement under belief of impending death. In a prosecution for homicide or in a civil action or proceeding, a statement made by a declarant, while believing that his or her death was imminent, concerning the cause or circumstances of what the declarant believed to be his or her impending death.

(3)   Statement against interest. A statement that was at the time of its making so far contrary to the declarant's pecuniary or proprietary interest, or so far tended to subject the declarant to civil or criminal liability, or to render invalid a claim by the declarant against another, that a reasonable person in the declarant's position would not have made the statement unless the declarant believed it to be true. A statement tending to expose the declarant to criminal liability, whether offered to exculpate or inculpate the accused, is not admissible unless corroborating circumstances clearly indicate the truthworthiness of the statement.

(4)   Statement of personal or family history.   (a) A statement concerning the declarant's own birth, adoption, marriage, divorce, legitimacy, relationship by blood, adoption, or marriage, ancestry, or other similar fact of personal or family history, even though the declarant had no means of acquiring personal knowledge of the matter stated; or (b) a statement concerning the foregoing matters, and death also, of another person, if the declarant was related to the other by blood, adoption, or marriage or was so intimately associated with the other's family as to be likely to have accurate information concerning the matter declared.

(5)   Statement by a deceased or incompetent person. The statement was made by a decedent or a mentally incompetent person, where all of the following apply:

(a) the estate or personal representative of the decedent's estate or the guardian or trustee of the incompetent person is a party;

(b) the statement was made before the death or the development of the incompetency;

(c)   the statement is offered to rebut testimony by an adverse party on a matter within the knowledge of the decedent or incompetent person.

(6)   Forfeiture by wrongdoing.   A statement offered against a party if the unavailability of the witness is due to the wrongdoing of the party for the purpose of preventing the witness from attending or testifying. However, a statement is not admissible under this rule unless the proponent has given to each adverse party advance written notice of an intention to introduce the statement sufficient to provide the adverse party a fair opportunity to contest the admissibility of the statement.

[Effective July 1, 1980; amended effective July 1, 1981, July 1, 1993; July 1, 2001.]

Staff Note (July 1, 2001 Amendment)

Evidence Rule 804   Hearsay exceptions; declarant unavailable
Evidence Rule 804(A) Definition of unavailability

The amendment to division (A) of the rule involved clarifying changes in language. In addition, the amendment placed in a separate paragraph what had been in the last sentence of division (A)(5) in order to clarify that the final sentence of the division applies to all of the rule's definitions of "unavailability." No substantive change is intended by these amendments.

Evidence Rule 804(B)(6)   Forfeiture by wrongdoing

The 2001 amendment added division (B)(6), forfeiture by wrongdoing. This division recognizes a forfeiture rule for hearsay statements that would have been admissible as testimony had the witness been present at trial. It is patterned on the federal rule, which was adopted in 1997. It codifies a principle that has been recognized at common-law in Ohio.

Rationale. The U.S. Supreme Court has recognized the forfeiture doctrine in the context of the right of confrontation. In *Illinois v. Allen*, 397 U.S. 337 (1970), the Court held that while the defendant has the right to be present at his or her trial, the right may be lost where defendant is so disorderly that the trial cannot be continued with his or her presence. Similarly, the Court held in *Taylor v. United States*, 414 U.S. 17 (1973), that defendant's voluntary absence from the courtroom can be construed as a waiver of the defendant's right to confrontation, without a warning from the court. In *Reynolds v. United States*, 98 U.S. 145 (1878), the Court upheld the admissibility of hearsay because the defendant had refused to reveal the declarant's location.

The term "forfeiture" was chosen over alternatives such as "waiver," "waiver by conduct," or "implied" or "constructive waiver" because the rule applies even if the party is not aware of the right of confrontation or the hearsay rule. In other words, the intentional relinquishment of a known right is *not* the standard.

Only a few Ohio cases have addressed the issue, but all have recognized that Ohio's common-law of evidence incorporates a rule of forfeiture similar to the federal rule. See *State v. Kilbane*, 1979 Ohio App. Lexis 10550, Nos. 38428, 38383, 38433 (8th Dist. Ct. App., 4/3/79), at *19; *State v. Liberatore*, 1983 Ohio App. Lexis 13808, No. 46784 (8th Dist. Ct. App. 12/3/83), at *13 ("[T]he evidence in *Steele* clearly indicated that the defendants had procured the witness' unavailability. The evidence in the instant case is far from clear that defendant procured Mata's 'unavailability'."); *State v. Brown*, 1986 Ohio App. Lexis 6567, No. 50505 (8th Dist. Ct. App. 4/24/86), at *11-12 ("[T]he victim expressed concern that the defendant's brother had threatened her mother and her children. An accused cannot rely on the confrontation clause to preclude extrajudicial evidence from a source which he obstructs.") See also *Steele v. Taylor*, 684 F.2d 1193, 1200-04 (6th Cir. 1982)(federal habeas corpus review of the conviction in *Kilbane*), cert. denied, 460 U.S. 1053 (1983).

Standard. The offering party must show (1) that the party engaged in wrongdoing that resulted in the witness's unavailability, and (2) that one purpose was to cause the witness to be unavailable at trial. See *United States v. Houlihan*, 92 F.3d 1271, 1279 (1st Cir. 1996) ("waiver by homicide") ("[I]t is sufficient in this regard to show that the evildoer was motivated *in part* by a desire to silence the witness; the intent to deprive the prosecution of testimony need not be the actor's *sole* motivation."), cert. denied, 519 U.S. 1118 (1997).

Coverage. As the federal drafters note, "[t]he wrongdoing need not consist of a criminal act. The rule applies to all parties, including the government. It applies to actions taken after the event to prevent a witness from testifying." Fed.R.Evid. 804 advisory committee's note. Thus, the rule does not apply to statements of the victim in a homicide prosecution concerning the homicide, including a felony-murder case.

The Ohio rule does not adopt the word "acquiesce" that is used in the federal rule. This departure from the federal model is intended to exclude from the rule's coverage situations in which, under federal practice, a party's mere inaction has been held to effect a forfeiture. See, e.g. *United States v. Mastrangelo*, 693 F.2d 269, 273-74 (2nd Cir. 1982), cert. denied, 467 U.S. 1204 (1984)("Bare knowledge of a plot to kill Bennett and a failure to give warning to appropriate authorities is sufficient to constitute a waiver.") Encouraging a witness to invoke a valid privilege, such as the Fifth Amendment, or the spousal competency rule, Evid. R. 601, does not trigger this rule because such conduct is not wrongdoing. Encouraging a witness to leave the state is wrongdoing in this context because no one has the legal right to refuse to provide testimony in the absence of a privilege or other rule of evidence. The prosecution, however, should not be able to cause a potential defense witness to assert the Fifth Amendment for the sole purpose of making that witness unavailable to the defense and then refuse to immunize that witness's testimony.

The rule extends to potential witnesses. See *United States v. Houlihan*, 92 F.3d 1271, 1279 (1st Cir. 1996) ("Although the reported cases all appear to involve actual witnesses, we can discern no principled reason why the waiver-by-misconduct doctrine should not apply with equal force if a defendant intentionally silences a *potential* witness.") (citation omitted), cert. denied, 519 U.S. 1118 (1997).

The rule governs only the hearsay aspect; the trial court retains authority under Evid. R. 403 to exclude unreliable statements. This is probably also a due process requirement. See generally Comment, The Admission of Hearsay Evidence Where Defendant Misconduct Causes the Unavailability of a Prosecution Witness, 43 Am. U. L. Rev. 995, 1014 (1994) ("The procuring defendant actually acknowledges the reliability of the absent witness' information when he or she endeavors to derail the witness' court appearance – an act the defendant would be less likely to commit if the witness's information is false or untrustworthy.")

The rule does not cover the admissibility of evidence regarding the wrongful act of procuring a witness's unavailability when the evidence is offered as an "implied" admission. Evidence of that character is not hearsay and is governed by the relevance rules. 1 Giannelli & Snyder, Baldwin's Ohio Practice, Evidence Section 401.9 (1996) (admissions by conduct).

Procedures. The trial court decides admissibility under Evid. R. 104(A); the traditional burden of persuasion (preponderance of evidence) rests with the party offering the evidence once an objection is raised. If the evidence is admitted, the court does not explain the basis of its ruling to the jury. This is similar to the procedure used in admitting a co-conspirator statement under Evid. R. 801(D)(2)(c), where the trial judge must decide the existence of a conspiracy as a condition of admissibility but would not inform the jury of this preliminary finding.

The opposing party would, however, have the opportunity to attack the reliability of the statement before the jury, Evid. R. 104(E), and impeach the declarant under Evid. R. 806.

The notice requirement, which is based on Evid. R. 609(B), may trigger an objection by a motion *in limine* and the opportunity for determining admissibility at a hearing outside the jury's presence. See *United States v. Thai*, 29 F.3d 785 (2d Cir. 1994) (unsworn statements made to detective prior to declarant's murder by defendant). ("Prior to admitting such testimony, the district court must hold a hearing in which the government has the burden of proving by a preponderance of the evidence that the defendant was responsible for the witness's absence.")

Staff Note (July 1, 1993 Amendment)

Rule 804 Hearsay Exceptions; Declarant Unavailable

Rule 804(A) Definition of unavailability

The only changes to division (A) are the use of gender neutral language; no substantive change is intended.

Rule 804(B) Hearsay exceptions

The substantive amendment to this division is in division (B)(5). The amendment to division (B)(5) removes references to "deaf-mutes" as a separate category of incompetent persons whose statements are admissible on behalf of an estate, guardian, or personal representative to rebut certain testimony by adverse parties.

The hearsay exception established by Evid. R. 804(B)(5) is designed to account for the effective abolition of the "Dead Man's Statute" (R.C. 2317.04) by the provisions of Evid. R. 601. The statute prohibited a party from testifying when the adverse party was, among others, "the guardian or trustee of either a deaf and dumb or an insane person." R.C. 2317.04. Under Evid. R. 601, there is no competency bar to a party's testimony in those cases, but if the party does testify, Evid. R. 804(B)(5) permits the guardian or trustee to introduce the statements of the ward in rebuttal.

As originally drafted, Evid. R. 804(B)(5) referred to the same categories of persons subject to guardianship as were referred to in the statute, albeit with some modernization in terminology. In particular, the rule identified "a deaf-mute who is now unable to testify" as a category of declarant-ward distinct from "a mentally incompetent person." As employed in the statute, however, that distinction appears to be no more than a remnant of nineteenth century guardianship laws, which at one time provided for the guardianship of the "deaf and dumb" separately from provisions for guardians of "idiots" or the "insane." See Act of March 9, 1838, Section 17, 36 Ohio Laws 40. To a large extent, provisions of that kind reflected the nineteenth century view that a person who was "deaf and dumb" was probably, if not certainly, mentally incompetent.

The nineteenth century's assumptions about the mental faculties of those with hearing or speech impairments are certainly inaccurate as an empirical matter. In any event, under modern law, the appointment of a guardian for an adult requires a determination that the person is mentally incompetent and there is no separate provision for the guardianship of incompetent "deaf-mutes." See R.C. 2111.02. That being the case, the "deaf-mute" declarants referred to in the rule are necessarily included within the rule's class of "mentally incompetent person[s]": an adult subject to a guardianship is by definition mentally incompetent, without regard to the existence of a "deaf-mute condition."

The identification of a separate class of "deaf-mute" declarants is thus redundant, and it likewise rests on archaic and mistaken views of the effect of hearing and speech impairments on one's mental capacities. The amendment deletes the rule's references to "deaf-mute" declarants in order to eliminate both of these difficulties, and in order to clarify that the rule applies only to statements by declarants who are deceased or mentally incompetent.

RULE 805.   Hearsay Within Hearsay

Hearsay included within hearsay is not excluded under the hearsay rule if each part of the combined statements conforms with an exception to the hearsay rule provided in these rules.

[Effective: July 1, 1980.]

RULE 806.   Attacking and Supporting Credibility of Declarant

(A)   When a hearsay statement, or a statement defined in Evid.R. 801(D)(2), (c), (d), or (e), has been admitted in evidence, the credibility of the declarant may be attacked, and if attacked may be supported, by any evidence that would be admissible for those purposes if declarant had testified as a witness.

(B)   Evidence of a statement or conduct by the declarant at any time, inconsistent with the declarant's hearsay statement, is not subject to any requirement that the declarant may have been afforded an opportunity to deny or explain.

(C)   Evidence of a declarant's prior conviction is not subject to any requirement that the declarant be shown a public record.

(D)   If the party against whom a hearsay statement has been admitted calls the declarant as a witness, the party is entitled to examine the declarant on the statement as if under cross-examination.

[Effective: July 1, 1980; amended July 1, 1998.]

Staff Note (July 1, 1998 Amendment)

Rule 806 Attacking and Supporting Credibility of Declarant

The content of divisions (A), (B), and (D) was part of the previous rule. These divisions were divided and lettered by the 1998 amendment, masculine references were made gender-neutral, and the style used for rule references was changed; no substantive change is intended.

Division (C) was added by the 1998 amendment. The limitation in Evid. R. 609(F) that the prior conviction be proved by the testimony of the witness or by public record shown to the witness during the examination clearly contemplates the witness's presence at trial; this is in tension with Evid. R. 806, which provides that a hearsay declarant may be impeached "by any evidence which would have been admissible for those purposes if declarant had testified as a witness." In *State v. Hatcher* (1996), 108 Ohio App.3d 628, 671 N.E.2d 572, a witness for the defense at the defendant's first trial was unavailable at the time of defendant's second trial. His testimony from the first trial was admitted into evidence as former testimony under Evid. R. 804(B)(1). The trial court then admitted into evidence certified copies of the declarant's prior felony convictions, which were offered by the prosecution to impeach the witness. The court of appeals noted the "arguable conflict" between Evid. R. 609(F) and Evid. R. 806, but determined that the admission of the certified copies of the witness's prior felony convictions was not error. The amendment clarifies this ambiguity; it does not change the requirements of Evid. R. 609(A) through (E) as applied to hearsay declarants.

RULE 807.   Hearsay Exceptions; Child Statements in Abuse Cases

(A)   An out-of-court statement made by a child who is under twelve years of age at the time of trial or hearing describing any sexual act performed by, with, or on the child or describing any act of physical violence directed against the child is not excluded as hearsay under Evid.R. 802 if all of the following apply:

(1)   The court finds that the totality of the circumstances surrounding the making of the statement provides particularized guarantees of trustworthiness that make the statement at least as reliable as statements admitted pursuant to Evid.R. 803 and 804. The circumstances must establish that the child was particularly likely to be telling the truth when the statement was made and that the test of cross-examination would add little to the reliability of the statement. In making its determination of the reliability of the statement, the court shall consider all of the circumstances surrounding the making of the statement, including but not limited to spontaneity, the internal consistency of the statement, the mental state of the child, the child's motive or lack of motive to fabricate, the child's use of terminology unexpected of a child of similar age, the means by which the statement was elicited, and the lapse of time between the act and the statement.   In making this determination, the court shall not consider whether there is independent proof of the sexual act or act of physical violence.

(2)   The child's testimony is not reasonably obtainable by the proponent of the statement.

(3)   There is independent proof of the sexual act or act of physical violence.

(4)   At least ten days before the trial or hearing, a proponent of the statement has notified all other parties in writing of the content of the statement, the time and place at which the statement was made, the identity of the witness who is to testify about the statement, and the circumstances surrounding the statement that are claimed to indicate its trustworthiness.

(B)   The child's testimony is "not reasonably obtainable by the proponent of the statement" under division (A)(2) of this rule only if one or more of the following apply:

(1)   The child refuses to testify concerning the subject matter of the statement or claims a lack of memory of the subject matter of the statement after a person trusted by the child, in the presence of the court, urges the child to both describe the acts described by the statement and to testify.

(2)   The court finds all of the following:

(a)   the child is absent from the trial or hearing;

(b)   the proponent of the statement has been unable to procure the child's attendance or testimony by process or other reasonable means despite a good faith effort to do so;

(c)   it is probable that the proponent would be unable to procure the child's testimony or attendance if the trial or hearing were delayed for a reasonable time.

(3)   The court finds both of the following:

(a)   the child is unable to testify at the trial or hearing because of death or then existing physical or mental illness or infirmity;

(b)   the illness or infirmity would not improve sufficiently to permit the child to testify if the trial or hearing were delayed for a reasonable time.

The proponent of the statement has not established that the child's testimony or attendance is not reasonably obtainable if the child's refusal, claim of lack of memory, inability, or absence is due to the procurement or wrongdoing of the proponent of the statement for the purpose of preventing the child from attending or testifying.

(C)   The court shall make the findings required by this rule on the basis of a hearing conducted outside the presence of the jury and shall make findings of fact, on the record, as to the bases for its ruling.

[Effective: July 1, 1991.]

Staff Note (July 1, 1991 Amendment)

Evid. R. 807 Hearsay Exceptions; Child Statements in Abuse Cases

The rule recognizes a hearsay exception for the statements of children in abuse situations. This exception is in addition to the exceptions enumerated in Evid. R. 803 and 804.

Many other jurisdictions have adopted child abuse hearsay exceptions. *See generally* Ringland, They Must Not Speak a Useless Word: The Case for a Children's Hearsay Exception for Ohio (1987), 14 Ohio N.U.L. Rev. 213. The Supreme Court in *State v. Boston* (1989), 46 Ohio St.3d 108, 545 N.E.2d 1220, asked the Rules Advisory Committee to review the subject. *See also* R.C. 2151.35(F).

Evid. R. 807(A) establishes four requirements for admission: (1) the statement must be trustworthy, (2) the child's testimony must be unavailable, (3) independent proof of the act must exist, and (4) the proponent must notify all other parties ten days before trial that such a statement will be offered in evidence. In addition, there are age and subject matter requirements: the child must be under 12 and the statement must relate to an act of sexual abuse or physical violence.

Rule 807(A)(1) Trustworthiness

Evid. R. 807(A)(1) codified the confrontation requirements specified by the United States Supreme Court in *Idaho v. Wright* (1990), 497 U.S. 805, 110 S.Ct. 3139, 111 L.Ed.2d 638. In *Wright*, the Court ruled that a child's statement admitted under a residual hearsay exception violated the Sixth Amendment where there were insufficient particularized guarantees of trustworthiness surrounding the making of the statement.

In determining trustworthiness, the Court adopted a "totality of the circumstances approach" and mentioned a number of factors: spontaneity and consistent repetition, mental state of the child, lack of motive to fabricate, and use of terminology unexpected of a child of similar age. These factors, as well as others, are specified in division (A)(1). The phrase "means by which the statement was elicited" concerns whether the statement was elicited by leading questions or after repeated promptings. Moreover, the time lapse between the act and the statement also is relevant in determining trustworthiness. The list of factors specified is not exhaustive. Additional factors, such as whether the statement was videotaped or whether the parents were involved in divorce or custody proceedings at the time the statement was made, may be relevant.

The last sentence of division (A)(1) provides that independent proof or corroboration of the statement is *not* a permissible factor in determining the trustworthiness of the statement. In *Wright*, the Supreme Court wrote: "the relevant circumstances include only those that surround the making of the statement and that render the declarant particularly worthy of belief." Under this approach, *corroboration* of the statement by independent evidence cannot be used to determine trustworthiness. The independent proof requirement in division (A)(3) is discussed below.

Rule 807(A)(2) and (B) Testimony not obtainable

Evid. R. 807(A)(2) requires the court to find that the child's testimony is not reasonably obtainable. Evid.R. 807(B) defines three circumstances that would satisfy this requirement. These circumstances are comparable to the unavailability requirements of Evid. R. 804(A); they have been modified to apply better to a child declarant. For example, a court would not have to specifically *order* the child to testify (as required for an adult under Evid. R. 804(A)(2)), provided the record clearly established a persistent refusal to testify.

In addition, a child who persisted in refusing to testify in a courtroom might be willing to testify via closed circuit television. *See* R.C. 2907.41; *Maryland v. Craig* (1990), 497 U.S. 836, 110 S.Ct. 3157, 111 L.Ed.2d 666. In such a circumstance, the child's testimony would be obtainable, albeit by closed-circuit television, and thus the hearsay statement would not be admissible under this rule.

Rule 807(A)(3) Independent proof

Although, under division (A)(1) and the *Wright* case, independent proof cannot be used to determine the trustworthiness of a hearsay statement, independent proof is a separate and additional requirement under division (A)(3) that must exist before a statement may be held admissible. This is comparable to the independent proof requirement of the co-conspirator exception, Evid. R. 801(D)(2)(e). The rule thus goes beyond the minimum Confrontation Clause requirements prescribed in *Wright*, as is permitted by *Wright*.

> "States are, of course, free, as a matter of state law, to demand corroboration of an unavailable child declarant's statements as well as other indicia of reliability before allowing the statement to be admitted into evidence." *Wright* at 3154 (Kennedy, J., dissenting).

Rule 807(A)(4) Notice

The pre-trial notice requirement is intended to alert opposing parties to the possible use of this exception, which in turn should trigger a request for an out-of-court hearing as required by Evid. R. 807(C).

Rule 807(C) Hearing and findings

Under Evid. R. 807(C), the admissibility determination must be made in a hearing conducted outside the presence of the jury. In addition, findings of fact supporting the court's ruling must be included in the record.

ARTICLE IX. AUTHENTICATION AND IDENTIFICATION

RULE 901.   Requirement of Authentication or Identification

(A)   General provision. The requirement of authentication or identification as a condition precedent to admissibility is satisfied by evidence sufficient to support a finding that the matter in question is what its proponent claims.

(B)   Illustrations. By way of illustration only, and not by way of limitation, the following are examples of authentication or identification conforming with the requirements of this rule:

(1)   Testimony of witness with knowledge. Testimony that a matter is what it is claimed to be.

(2)   Nonexpert opinion on handwriting. Nonexpert opinion as to the genuineness of handwriting, based upon familiarity not acquired for purposes of the litigation.

(3)   Comparison by trier or expert witness. Comparison by the trier of fact or by expert witness with specimens which have been authenticated.

(4)   Distinctive characteristics and the like. Appearance, contents, substance, internal patterns, or other distinctive characteristics, taken in conjunction with circumstances.

(5)   Voice identification. Identification of a voice, whether heard firsthand or through mechanical or electronic transmission or recording, by opinion based upon hearing the voice at any time under circumstances connecting it with the alleged speaker.

(6)   Telephone conversations. Telephone conversations, by evidence that a call was made to the number assigned at the time by the telephone company to a particular person or business, if (a) in the case of a person, circumstances, including self-identification, show the person answering to be the one called, or (b) in the case of a business, the call was made to a place of business and the conversation related to business reasonably transacted over the telephone.

(7)   Public records or reports. Evidence that a writing authorized by law to be recorded or filed and in fact recorded or filed in a public office, or a purported public record, report, statement or data compilation, in any form, is from the public office where items of this nature are kept.

(8)   Ancient documents or data compilation. Evidence that a document or data compilation, in any form, (a) is in such condition as to create no suspicion concerning its authenticity, (b) was in a place where it, if authentic, would likely be, and (c) has been in existence twenty years or more at the time it is offered.

(9)   Process or system. Evidence describing a process or system used to produce a result and showing that the process or system produces an accurate result.

(10)   Methods provided by statute or rule. Any method of authentication or identification provided by statute enacted by the General Assembly not in conflict with a rule of the Supreme Court of Ohio or by other rules prescribed by the Supreme Court.

[Effective: July 1, 1980.]

RULE 902.   Self-Authentication

Extrinsic evidence of authenticity as a condition precedent to admissibility is not required with respect to the following:

(1)   Domestic public documents under seal. A document bearing a seal purporting to be that of the United States, or of any State, district, Commonwealth, territory, or insular possession thereof, or the Panama Canal Zone, or the Trust Territory of the Pacific Islands, or of a political subdivision, department, officer, or agency thereof, and a signature purporting to be an attestation or execution.

(2)   Domestic public documents not under seal. A document purporting to bear the signature in the official capacity of an officer or employee of any entity included in paragraph (1) hereof, having no seal, if a public officer having a seal and having official duties in the district or political subdivision of the officer or employee certifies under seal that the signer has the official capacity and that the signature is genuine.

(3)   Foreign public documents. A document purporting to be executed or attested in the official capacity by a person authorized by the laws of a foreign country to make the execution or attestation, and accompanied by a final certification as to the genuineness of the signature and official position (a) of the executing or attesting person, or (b) of any foreign official whose certificate of genuineness of signature and official position relates to the execution or attestation or is in a chain of certificates of genuineness of signature and official position relating to the execution or attestation. A final certification may be made by a secretary of embassy or legation, consul general, consul, vice consul, or consular agent of the United States, or a diplomatic or consular official of the foreign country assigned or accredited to the United States. If reasonable opportunity has been given to all parties to investigate the authenticity and accuracy of official documents, the court may, for good cause shown, order that they be treated as presumptively authentic without final certification or permit them to be evidenced by an attested summary with or without final certification.

(4)   Certified copies of public records. A copy of an official record or report or entry therein, or of a document authorized by law to be recorded or filed and actually recorded or filed in a public office, including data compilations in any form, certified as correct by the custodian or other person authorized to make the certification, by certificate complying with paragraph (1), (2), or (3) of this rule or complying with any law of a jurisdiction, state or federal, or rule prescribed by the Supreme Court of Ohio.

(5)   Official publications. Books, pamphlets, or other publications purporting to be issued by public authority.

(6)   Newspapers and periodicals. Printed materials purporting to be newspapers or periodicals, including notices and advertisements contained therein.

(7)   Trade inscriptions and the like. Inscriptions, signs, tags, or labels purporting to have been affixed in the course of business and indicating ownership, control, or origin.

(8)   Acknowledged documents. Documents accompanied by a certificate of acknowledgment executed in the manner provided by law by a notary public or other officer authorized by law to take acknowledgments.

(9)   Commercial paper and related documents. Commercial paper, signatures thereon, and documents relating thereto to the extent provided by general commercial law.

(10)   Presumptions created by law. Any signature, document, or other matter declared by any law of a jurisdiction, state or federal, to be presumptively or prima facie genuine or authentic.

[Effective: July 1, 1980; amended effectively July 1, 2007.]

RULE 903.   Subscribing Witness' Testimony Unnecessary

The testimony of a subscribing witness is not necessary to authenticate a writing unless required by the laws of the jurisdiction whose laws govern the validity of the writing.

[Effective: July 1, 1980.]

ARTICLE X. CONTENTS OF WRITINGS, RECORDINGS AND PHOTOGRAPHS

RULE 1001. Definitions

For purposes of this article the following definitions are applicable:

(1) **Writings and recordings.** "Writings" and "recordings" consist of letters, words, or numbers, or their equivalent, set down by handwriting, typewriting, printing, photostating, photographing, magnetic impulse, mechanical or electronic recording, or other forms of data compilation.

(2) **Photographs.** "Photographs" include still photographs, X-ray films, video tapes, and motion pictures.

(3) **Original.** An "original" of a writing or recording is the writing or recording itself or any counterpart intended to have the same effect by a person executing or issuing it. An "original" of a photograph includes the negative or any print therefrom. If data are stored in a computer or similar device, any printout or other output readable by sight, shown to reflect the data accurately, is an "original."

(4) **Duplicate.** A "duplicate" is a counterpart produced by the same impression as the original, or from the same matrix, or by means of photography, including enlargements and miniatures, or by mechanical or electronic re-recording, or by chemical reproduction, or by other equivalent techniques which accurately reproduce the original. A "duplicate" includes a counterpart from which personal identifiers have been omitted pursuant to Rule 45 of the Rules of Superintendence for the Courts of Ohio, and which otherwise accurately reproduces the original.

[Effective: July 1, 1980, amended effectively July 1, 2012.]

RULE 1002. Requirement of Original

To prove the content of a writing, recording, or photograph, the original writing, recording, or photograph is required, except as otherwise provided in these rules or by statute enacted by the General Assembly not in conflict with a rule of the Supreme Court of Ohio.

[Effective: July 1, 1980.]

RULE 1003. Admissibility of Duplicates

A duplicate is admissible to the same extent as an original unless (1) a genuine question is raised as to the authenticity of the original or (2) in the circumstances it would be unfair to admit the duplicate in lieu of the original.

[Effective: July 1, 1980.]

RULE 1004. Admissibility of Other Evidence of Contents

The original is not required, and other evidence of the contents of a writing, recording, or photograph is admissible if:

(1)   **Originals lost or destroyed.** All originals are lost or have been destroyed, unless the proponent lost or destroyed them in bad faith; or

(2)   **Original not obtainable.** No original can be obtained by any available judicial process or procedure; or

(3)   **Original in possession of opponent.** At a time when an original was under the control of the party against whom offered, that party was put on notice, by the pleadings or otherwise, that the contents would be subject of proof at the hearing, and that party does not produce the original at the hearing; or

(4)   **Collateral matters.** The writing, recording, or photograph is not closely related to a controlling issue.

[Effective: July 1, 1980; amended effectively July 1, 2007.]

RULE 1005. Public Records

The contents of an official record, or of a document authorized to be recorded or filed and actually recorded or filed, including data compilations in any form if otherwise admissible, may be proved by copy, certified as correct in accordance with Rule 902, Civ.R. 44, Crim.R. 27 or testified to be correct by a witness who has compared it with the original. If a copy which complies with the foregoing cannot be obtained by the exercise of reasonable diligence, then other evidence of the contents may be given.

[Effective: July 1, 1980.]

RULE 1006. Summaries

The contents of voluminous writings, recordings, or photographs which cannot conveniently be examined in court may be presented in the form of a chart, summary, or calculation. The originals, or duplicates, shall be made available for examination or copying, or both, by other parties at a reasonable time and place. The court may order that they be produced in court.

[Effective: July 1, 1980.]

RULE 1007. Testimony or Written Admission of Party

Contents of writings, recordings, or photographs may be proved by the testimony or deposition of the party against whom offered or by that party's written admission, without accounting for the nonproduction of the original.

[Effective: July 1, 1980; amended effectively July 1, 2007.]

RULE 1008. Functions of Court and Jury

When the admissibility of other evidence of contents of writings, recordings, or photographs under these rules depends upon the fulfillment of a condition of fact, the question whether the condition has been fulfilled is ordinarily for the court to determine in accordance with the provisions of Rule 104. However, when an issue is raised (a) whether the asserted writing ever existed, or (b) whether another writing, recording, or photograph produced at the trial is the original, or (c) whether other evidence of contents correctly reflects the contents, the issue is for the trier of fact to determine as in the case of other issues of fact.

[Effective: July 1, 1980.]

ARTICLE XI. MISCELLANEOUS RULES

RULE 1101.   [RESERVED]

RULE 1102. Effective Date

(A)   Effective date of rules. These rules shall take effect on the first day of July, 1980. They govern all proceedings in actions brought after they first take effect and also all further proceedings in actions then pending, except to the extent that in the opinion of the court their application in a particular action pending when the rules take effect would not be feasible or would work injustice, in which event former evidentiary rules apply.

(B)   Effective date of amendments. The amendments submitted by the Supreme Court to the General Assembly on January 14, 1981, and on April 29, 1981, shall take effect on July 1, 1981. They govern all further proceedings in actions then pending, except to the extent that their application in a particular action pending when the amendments take effect would not be feasible or would work injustice, in which event the former procedure applies.

(C)   Effective date of amendments. The amendments submitted by the Supreme Court to the General Assembly on January 12, 1990, and further revised and submitted on April 16, 1990, shall take effect on July 1, 1990. They govern all proceedings in actions brought after they take effect and also all further proceedings in actions then pending, except to the extent that their application in a particular action pending when the amendments take effect would not be feasible or would work injustice, in which event the former procedure applies.

(D)   Effective Date of Amendments. The amendments submitted by the Supreme Court to the General Assembly on January 10, 1991 and further revised and submitted on April 29, 1991, shall take effect on July 1, 1991. They govern all proceedings in actions brought after they take effect and also all further proceedings in actions then pending, except to the extent that their application in a particular action pending when the amendments take effect would not be feasible or would work injustice, in which event the former procedure applies.

(E)   Effective date of amendments. The amendments filed by the Supreme Court with the General Assembly on January 14, 1992 and further filed on April 30, 1992, shall take effect on July 1, 1992. They govern all proceedings in actions brought after they take effect and also all further proceedings in actions then pending, except to the extent that their application in a particular action pending when the amendments take effect would not be feasible or would work injustice, in which event the former procedure applies.

(F)   Effective date of amendments. The amendments submitted by the Supreme Court to the General Assembly on January 8, 1993 and further filed on April 30, 1993 shall take effect on July 1, 1993. They govern all proceedings in actions brought after they take effect and also all further proceedings in actions then pending, except to the extent that their application in a particular action pending when the amendments take effect would not be feasible or would work injustice, in which event the former procedure applies.

(G)   Effective date of amendments. The amendments submitted by the Supreme Court to the General Assembly on January 14, 1994 and further filed on April 29, 1994 shall take effect on July 1, 1994. They govern all proceedings in actions brought after they take effect and also all further proceedings in actions then pending, except to the extent that their application in a particular action pending when the amendments take effect would not be feasible or would work injustice, in which event the former procedure applies.

(H)   Effective date of amendments. The amendments to Rules 101, 102, and 403 filed by the Supreme Court with the General Assembly on January 5, 1996 and refiled on April 26, 1996 shall take effect on July 1, 1996. They govern all proceedings in actions brought after they take effect and also all further proceedings in actions then pending, except to the extent that their application in a particular action pending when the amendments take effect would not be feasible or would work injustice, in which event the former procedure applies.

(I)   Effective date of amendments. The amendments to Rules 607, 613, 616, 706, and 806 filed by the Supreme Court with the General Assembly on January 15, 1998 and further revised and refiled on April 30, 1998 shall take effect on July 1, 1998. They govern all proceedings in actions brought after they take effect and also all further proceedings in actions then pending, except to the extent that their application in a particular action pending when the amendments take effect would not be feasible or would work injustice, in which event the former procedure applies.

(J)   Effective date of amendments. The amendments to Rules 101 and 1102(I) filed by the Supreme Court with the General Assembly on January 13, 1999 shall take effect on July 1, 1999. They govern all proceedings in actions brought after they take effect and also all further proceedings in actions then pending, except to the extent that their application in a particular action pending when the amendments take effect would not be feasible or would work injustice, in which event the former procedure applies.

(K)   Effective date of amendments. The amendments to Evidence Rule 407 filed by the Supreme Court with the General Assembly on January 13, 2000 and refiled on April 27, 2000 shall take effect on July 1, 2000. They govern all proceedings in actions brought after they take effect and also all further proceedings in actions then pending, except to the extent that their application in a particular action pending when the amendments take effect would not be feasible or would work injustice, in which event the former procedure applies.

(L)   Effective date of amendments. The amendments to Evidence Rules 615 and 804 filed by the Supreme Court with the General Assembly on January 12, 2001, and refiled on April 26, 2001, shall take effect on July 1, 2001. They govern all proceedings in actions brought after they take effect and also all further proceedings in actions then pending, except to the extent that their application in a particular action pending when the amendments take effect would not be feasible or would work injustice, in which event the former procedure applies.

(M)   Effective date of amendments. The amendments to Evidence Rules 609 and 615 filed by the Supreme Court with the General Assembly on January 9, 2003 and refiled on April 28, 2003, shall take effect on July 1, 2003. They govern all proceedings in actions brought after they take effect and also all further proceedings in actions then pending, except to the extent that their application in a particular action pending when the amendments take effect would not be feasible or would work injustice, in which event the former procedure applies.

(N)   Effective date of amendments. The amendment to Evidence Rule 803 and the repeal of Evidence Rule 706 filed by the Supreme Court with the General Assembly on January 12, 2006 shall take effect on July 1, 2006. The amendment and repeal govern all proceedings in actions brought after they take effect and also all further proceedings in actions then pending, except to the extent that their application in a particular action pending when the amendments take effect would not be feasible or would work injustice, in which event the former procedure applies.

(O)   Effective date of amendments. The amendments to the Rules of Evidence filed by the Supreme Court with the General Assembly on January 11, 2007 and refiled April 30, 2007 shall take effect on July 1, 2007. They govern all proceedings in actions brought after they take effect and also all further proceedings in actions then pending, except to the extent that their application in a particular action pending when the amendments take effect would not be feasible or would work injustice, in which event the former procedure applies.

(P)   Effective date of amendments. The amendments to the Rules of Evidence filed by the Supreme Court with the General Assembly on January 5, 2011 and refiled on April 21, 2011 shall take effect on July 1, 2011. They govern all proceedings in actions brought after they take effect and also all further proceedings in actions then pending, except to the extent that their application in a particular action pending when the amendments take effect would not be feasible or would work injustice, in which event the former procedure applies.

(Q)   Effective date of amendments. The amendments to the Rules of Evidence filed by the Supreme Court with the General Assembly on January 13, 2012 and refiled on April 30, 2012 shall take effect on July 1, 2012. They govern all proceedings in actions brought after they take effect and also all further proceedings in actions then pending, except to the extent that their application in a particular action pending when the amendments take effect would not be feasible or would work injustice, in which event the former procedure applies.

(R)   Effective date of amendments. The amendments to the Rules of Evidence 601, 803, and 1102 filed by the Supreme Court with the General Assembly on January 13, 2016 and refiled on April 29, 2016 shall take effect on July 1, 2016. They govern all proceedings in actions brought after they take effect and also all further proceedings in actions then pending, except to the extent that their application in a particular action pending when the amendments take effect would not be feasible or would work injustice, in which event the former procedure applies.

(S)   Effective date of amendments. The amendments to the Rules of Evidence 103 filed by the Supreme Court with the General Assembly on January 6, 2017 and refiled on April

26, 2017 shall take effect on July 1, 2017. They govern all proceedings in actions brought after they take effect and also all further proceedings in actions then pending, except to the extent that their application in a particular action pending when the amendments take effect would not be feasible or would work injustice, in which event the former procedure applies.

Staff Note (July 1, 2007 Amendments)

The 2007 amendments to the Ohio Rules of Evidence make no substantive changes to the rules. The rules are amended to apply gender neutral language.

Staff Note (July 1, 1999 Amendment)

Rule 1102 Effective Date

Division (I) of this rule, governing rules and amendments that took effect July 1, 1998, was amended to delete an erroneous reference to Rule 611 of the Rules of Evidence. Evid. R. 611 was not amended in 1998 and the reference to it was deleted from division (I).

RULE 1103. Title

These rules shall be known as the Ohio Rules of Evidence and may be cited as "Evidence Rules" or "Evid.R. ____."

[Effective: July 1, 1980.]